WORK HARD
AND
YOU
SHALL BE
REWARDED

WORK HARD
AND
YOU
SHALL BE
REWARDED

Urban Folklore from
the Paperwork Empire

Alan Dundes
and
Carl R. Pagter

 WAYNE STATE UNIVERSITY PRESS   DETROIT

398.20973 DUNDES 1992

Dundes, Alan.

Work hard and you shall be rewarded : urban folklore

Copyright © 1975 by Alan Dundes and Carl R. Pagter.
Copyright © 1992 by Wayne State University Press, Detroit, Michigan 48202.

Originally published as Volume 62 in the American Folklore Society's Memoir Series, William Hugh Jansen, General Editor.

Manufactured in the United States of America

96 95 94 93 92   5 4 3 2 1

Library of Congress Cataloging-in-Publication Data

Dundes, Alan.
    [Urban folklore from the paperwork empire]
    Work hard and you shall be rewarded : urban folklore from the paperwork
empire / Alan Dundes & Carl R. Pagter.
        p.   cm.
    Previously published: Bloomington : Indiana University, 1978, c1975. With new
pref.
    ISBN 0-8143-2432-0 (pbk. : alk. paper)
    1. Office practice—United States—Folklore. 2. Urban folklore—United States. 3.
American wit and humor. 4. United States—Social life and customs—1971-   I.
Pagter, Carl R., 1934-
II. title.
    [GR105.D86   1992]
    398.2'0973'091732—dc20   92-11158
                                                                          CIP

Cover Design by Joanne Elkin Kinney

CONTENTS

PREFACE

Little did we realize in 1970 when we completed the first draft of *Work Hard and You Shall Be Rewarded* the magnitude and scope of the materials transmitted by office copier. In retrospect, we can see that the 96 items we collected in the late 1960s and early 1970s barely scratched the surface of this facinating and fast-growing tradition. At that time, such items had not yet been recognized as bona fide folklore—in part because they were written rather than oral. That was undoubtedly one reason why it took five years to find a publisher for the manuscript. Another was that the uncensored nature of this folklore was offensive to one group or another.

In 1975, the American Folklore Society authorized the publication of the volume in its Memoir series, thanks in large measure to the courage of its editor, the late Wm. Hugh Jansen. (One of the reviewers who had recommended publication of our work was Ben Botkin we later learned.) The University of Texas Press, then the contractual publisher of American Folklore Society Publications, declined to put its imprint on the book, so the only clue to the identity of the publisher was the post office box number in Austin, Texas that appeared on the plain brown wrapper chosen to cover the book. Although the first printing sold out the same year in which it was published, the Press did not feel comfortable reprinting the book unless certain items were deleted from it. As editors we protested, and the cloth edition was reprinted twice more. The University of Texas Press was not interested in issuing a paperback edition, and it was not until 1978 that Indiana

University Press published the book in that form, which went through another four reprintings.

In the meantime, we continued our collecting efforts, greatly assisted by individuals around the country who were kind enough to share with us their examples of photocopier folklore. By 1978, we had completed a second volume entitled *When You're Up To Your Ass in Alligators*, which contained an additional 138 items. Again we were disappointed in our attempts to find a publisher for this work. Indiana University Press declined it, believing the first volume had exhausted the subject matter and the public interest in such folklore. (One wonders what impact this philosophy of publishing might have had on such earlier multi-volume collections of folklore such as the Grimm tales or the Child ballads!) Fortunately, Wayne State University Press recognized the importance and value of these traditional materials and published our second volume nearly ten years after we had completed it. Encouraged by Wayne State, we embarked upon a third sampling that was by far the most extensive to date, consisting of 235 individual items. This was published in 1991 under the title *Never Try To Teach A Pig To Sing*. With this re-publication of *Work Hard*, nearly 500 items of photocopier folklore are available from a single source.

We are gratified to know that our initial volume sparked research elsewhere in the world. Collections of cognate texts from Denmark, England, Germany, and Sweden have attested to the international distribution of many of the items first reported in this book. Moreover, the technological development of improved means of rapid communication such as telephone facsimile ("FAX") or electronic mail ("E-mail") has resulted in the increased dissemination of these and other materials. Such inventions have surely stimulated the creation of "new" xerographic folklore and made it plausible to speak of "folklore by FAX."

We have chosen not to revise or update the texts, commentary, or introduction of the original volume, but we might note here that we feel the battle to establish the authenticity of these written materials as folklore has been won. No one disputes the identification of these items as folklore and the old-fashioned definitional criterion of "orality" has been successfully called into question. Most readers of this volume will recognize a fair number of the items included as still being actively circulated. This should affirm that their content remains relevant to contemporary American life.

We thank Wayne State University Press for ensuring that this unusual collection of traditional Americana will continue to be available to scholars as well as to a new generation of readers who we trust will be instructed and entertained by these truly remarkable materials.

PREFACE TO THE FIRST EDITION

This unusual collection of modern urban folklore has come about through the collaboration of a university professor of folklore and a practicing attorney whose avocation is folksinging. The majority of the materials are of the type that many people may have seen at one time or another but that are extremely difficult to locate at any given instant. Certainly, the materials included in this book have not hitherto been easily available in published form. We believe the present compilation to be unique and we hope valuable to serious students of American culture.

The compilers wish to thank the many students and colleagues who were kind enough to contribute individual items for consideration. Although it is impossible to mention all those who helped ferret out exemplars, the compilers would like to express their appreciation to the following: Barbara Alderson, Diana Artel, Gary Bogue, Jess Burch, Cheri Coulter, Hal T. Curtis, Oscar Curtis, Jeannette Eberhard, Harry Ellis, Brian Eukel, Dorel French, Marven Gibson, Garrett Grant, Laurie Haig, Thomas D. Hall, Scott Hambly, Julia Hernandez, Sharon Heuga, Joseph Hickerson, William Holt, LeClair Keating, Barbara Kirshenblatt-Gimblett, James Kaufman, Linda Krock, Sally Leipzig, Peter Lovett, Mary-Ann Lutzker, Neil McCallum, Dennis McDonald, Joyce McMaster, Timothy M. Moore, Michael Nisley, Gail Potts, Bruce Radde, John Sandy, Gerald Sena, Bob and Ruth Sicular, Patricia L. Smith, Paul and Mary Strong, Aili Sumeri, Peter Tamony, Marvell C. Tingle, Kenneth M. Turner, Christine Van Wart, Margretta von Sothen, Joy Watts, and Constance Wiggen.

To Carolyn Dundes and Linda Pagter, the compilers owe the inspiration required to complete what had started originally as a labor of love. A special vote of thanks is also due those same ladies for successfully resisting the great temptation of touching a match to the finished manuscript. Finally, the compilers would like to dedicate the book to all the office workers of the world without whom there would be no folklore from the paperwork empire.

INTRODUCTION

Urban folklore from the paperwork empire represents part of the human response to some of the ills of urban life. Anyone who has ever been rebuffed by a form letter will be able to appreciate the urban folklore found in this study. Yet, despite the widespread popularity of most of the items reported here, serious consideration of these fascinating and unusual materials has not yet taken place.

In conventional anthropology and folklore scholarship, great value is still placed upon the collection of raw data. Theories and methods come and go, often enjoying several years of faddish favor before joining predecessors in the overflowing dustbin of discarded "new" approaches. But good data never go out of style. Each generation of scholars, while it may poke fun at straw-men theorists of previous times, often has reason to be grateful to those very same theorists for data they gathered so assiduously. Obsolete theories may prove of some interest to those few members of a discipline who serve as its historians, but somehow data never lose their freshness and excitement. A folktale accurately recorded a century ago is no less valuable than one collected today.

The present study is first and foremost a collection of texts. In that sense, it represents part of the longstanding effort to record as many of the products of the human imagination as possible. However, this collection of texts is not like any collection of folklore previously assembled. Let us attempt to explain why the data are so unique.

Were this study entitled "More Mohave Myths" or "Still More

Yoruba Proverbs," no reputable academic publisher or audience would question its appropriateness for publication. Texts of Mohave myths or Yoruba proverbs, even if presented with no analysis whatsoever, are recognized as valuable cultural documents, the collection and study of which fall clearly within the purview of the anthropological folklorist. The texts in the present compilation, however, come from American society, and, unfortunately, texts from one's own society tend to be regarded frequently much like prophets, that is, without honor. Yet it should be obvious that, if folkloristic texts from *other* societies are deemed valuable, why shouldn't texts from one's own be accorded similar status? One historical reason for the disparity is suggested by a fundamental difference between the disciplines of anthropology and folklore.

Anthropologists, generally speaking, have been primarily concerned with studying other cultures and not their own. In contrast, folklorists have typically been engaged in studying their own cultures or selected segments of their own societies, for instance, the rural, uneducated "peasants" or "folk" groups. Thus, American anthropologists would by definition be interested in Mohave or Yoruba texts, but would not necessarily be concerned with texts from American society. Fortunately, a recent change in attitude in anthropological circles has encouraged students of anthropology to study their own societies. Part of this shift may be attributed to the fact that anthropologists are no longer so welcome or, should we say, tolerated among some peoples of the world. The death knell of colonialism has sounded for academic colonialism as well. Third-world peoples in particular are tired of being studied by uninvited visiting anthropologists. Declarations in various countries to the effect that anthropologists are personae non gratae have virtually forced anthropologists to consider seriously areas of study closer to home. In any event, American studies is just beginning to become one of the areas of specialization in graduate studies in anthropology.

If we can understand why anthropologists have been slow to study the kinds of materials reported in the present study, why is it, one may legitimately ask, that folklorists—who do study their own cultures—have failed to consider this type of data? The answer lies, we believe, in folklorists' overly narrow definition of both "folk" and "lore."

The concept of folk as employed by folklorists in Europe normally refers either to a lower stratum of society (*vulgus in populo*) or to an old-fashioned, backward segment within a so-called civilized society. Frequently, the criterion of literacy was a factor in the definition of folk. Specifically, the folk could not read or write. In this light the folk was defined as the illiterate in a literate society. Societies without a written language did not, according to this definition, qualify as folk at all. Such societies, variously ethnocentrically labeled as preliterate, nonliterate, primitive, or savage, were not folk, and for this reason even today the art or the music of the American Indian is rarely, if ever, referred to as folk art or folk music. Rather they fall under the academic rubric of "primitive" art or music. In the present context, the exclusion of peoples without a form of writing was no more absurd than the exclusion of peoples who could write. One should realize that, in the strict definition of "folk," there could be no such thing as "urban" folklore. Urban folklore would be a contradiction in terms. In fact, "folk" and "urban" were and indeed still are thought to be at opposite ends of a theoretical continuum. In this framework, folk society is synonymous with "peasant" society; peasants moving into the city become urbanized and lose their status as "folk." To speak of "urban folklore" is to utter nonsense in the context of the traditional definition of "folk."

The modern definition of folk as any group whatsoever that shares at least one common factor—language, occupation, religion, ethnicity—makes it possible to consider the folklore of various urban groups. Labor unions, industrial companies, civil-rights groups, and hippies are all examples of urban folk groups who have their own special sets of traditions. The "folk" that is in part defined by the present corpus of data presumably includes nearly every American who has ever had occasion to work in an office or who has ever had some confrontation with a form of modern bureaucracy.

If American folklorists have been willing to extend the rather limited nineteenth-century concept of "folk" as peasant, they have not been equally flexible in their reconsideration of one of the crucial alleged criteria of "lore," namely, the necessity of its having been transmitted orally. American folklorists appear to be united in their virtually unanimous agreement that folklore, by definition, refers to materials *orally transmitted*. We disagree with this criterion, and it is our hope that publication of the present study will put an end to this misconception once and for all. Nearly all the materials contained in our corpus are transmitted by other than oral means. These means include hand copying, typewriting, photocopying, and xerography. We intend to demonstrate that the materials are truly folklore and accordingly that the longstanding "oral" definition of folklore must at least be amended if not scrapped altogether.

For the benefit of those readers who may not be familiar with the history of American folklore scholarship, we should like to establish that the "oral" criterion has been and continues to be a critical modus operandi for professional folklorists. In 1890, for instance, we find the following unequivocal statement made by W. W. Newell, one of the founders of the American Folklore Society in 1888 and the first editor of the *Journal of American Folklore*: "By folk-lore is to be understood oral tradition—information and belief handed down from generation to generation without the use of writing."[1]

But that was 1890! In considering more modern views, we find the same bias. Among numerous similar statements to be found in the entry "folklore" in the *Standard Dictionary of Folklore, Mythology and Legend*, we select three. (We have italicized the key words in the following remarks by Melville J. Herskovits, William R. Bascom, and Archer Taylor.)

. . . folklore has come more and more to denote the study of the *unwritten* literature of any group. . .

In anthropological usage, the term folklore has come to mean myths, legends, folktales, proverbs, riddles, verse, and a variety of other forms of artistic

---

[1] W. W. Newell, "The Study of Folklore," *Transactions of the New York Academy of Sciences* 9 (1890): 134-136.

expression whose medium is the *spoken* word.

It is usual to define folklore either literally as the lore of the folk or, more descriptively, in terms of an *oral* literature tradition.[2]

These statements are not in the least atypical. One can find nearly identical statements made by any leading American folklorist. Stith Thompson makes the following distinction: "We can, of course, make the differentiation between certain groups of folklorists into those who give a broad interpretation and those who give a narrow interpretation of the field. My impression is that most folklorists in the United States belong to the narrow-interpretation group. They are likely to think of folklore as having something to do with the *spoken* word."[3]

Richard M. Dorson also adopts the oral criterion: " 'Folklore' usually suggests the *oral* traditions channeled across the centuries through human mouths. . . . In the United States, folklore has customarily meant the *spoken* and sung traditions."[4]

Francis Lee Utley, in an entire essay devoted to the vexing and troublesome matter of defining folklore, finally boils it all down to "literature orally transmitted." Although folklorist Utley does at least allow that urban groups may have folklore, he does insist upon the "oral transmission" criterion: "For my own operation, I will stand by the very simple statement that folk literature is *orally* transmitted literature wherever found, among primitive isolates, or civilized marginal cultures, urban or rural cultures, dominant or subordinate groups. The heuristic value of *'orally transmitted,'* our key phrase, is great"[5]

In view of the above consensus, it should come as no surprise

---

[2] Maria Leach, ed., *Standard Dictionary of Folklore, Mythology and Legend*, vol. 1 (New York: Funk & Wagnalls, 1972).

[3] Stith Thompson, *Four Symposia on Folklore* (Bloomington: Indiana University Press, 1953), p. 255. Emphasis added.

[4] Richard M. Dorson, *American Folklore* (Chicago: University of Chicago Press, 1959), p. 2. Emphasis added.

[5] Francis Lee Utley, "Folk Literature: An Operational Definition," *Journal of American Folklore* 74 (1961): 193-206. Emphasis added.

to find that a very recent textbook used in teaching folklore at the college level employs the same criterion: "Although others use the term 'folklore' with different meanings, ranging from children's literature to rumor and hearsay, it is in the scholarly sense of *'oral tradition'* that we will employ the word here."[6]

This admittedly brief discussion should be sufficient to demonstrate that "oral transmission" is considered to be not just one of the critical criteria in the definition of folklore, but indeed one of the most important criteria if not *the* most important criterion utilized by American folklorists. It is in this light that the reader should judge one of the purposes of the present study, namely, to question this basic premise of American folklore scholarship. In order to challenge successfully this longstanding tradition, we must prove (1) that the materials we include are bona fide folklore, and (2) that they are transmitted by nonoral means.

The second point is easy enough to establish. The materials included herein are rarely if ever transmitted orally. Certainly, the folk cartoons can hardly be said to circulate by purely oral means. But even the verbal materials tend to move from person to person by means of copying. In the last several decades, the means of rapid copying of texts have become increasingly available to a wide segment of the public. Not only does every major office have some form of copy service, but inexpensive public commercial facilities also make it possible for any individual to copy any page at a nominal cost. (To the extent that even small towns possess such copying facilities, the folklore produced and transmitted thereby becomes not just urban folklore but general American folklore.) There is little question that the items contained in this study are circulated primarily by individuals making copies for friends by running their own copies through the nearest photocopier.

But are these items folklore? We submit that they are. They are traditional insofar as they manifest "multiple existence," one of the principal characteristics of a folklore form. These items exist in multiple versions and in more than one time or place—just as all folklore does. A poem written by a poet or a song written by a

[6] Jan Harold Brunvand, *The Study of American Folklore* (New York: W. W. Horton, 1968), p. 2. Emphasis added.

composer is not a folk poem or folksong unless or until it exists in at least two or more places.

One result of multiple existence is variation, another indication that one is dealing with folkloristic material. As an item moves from person to person, change is almost inevitable. Each person (and ultimately each society) makes the item of folklore his own by consciously or unconsciously placing his personal interpretative stamp upon it. Whereas the text of a literary poem is presumably the same each time one reads it, the text of a folksong is never exactly the same. Each version of a folksong is "just a little bit different" from any other version. This differentness is amply demonstrated in the versions of folk cartoons in this study. Whereas one might think that an individual might be content merely to copy a cartoon via xerox and leave it at that, it is clear that individuals take the time and trouble to redraw traditional cartoons. Yet the versions are similar enough to show genetic interrelationships.

The materials contained in this study are traditional: they manifest multiple existence in space and time, and they exist in variant forms. Without burdening the reader with all the variants of each item, we have tried nonetheless to signal some of the range of variation in each case. Except for the oral criterion, these materials would doubtless pass muster as folklore for most American folklorists. Had we lied and claimed that we had elicited all of the texts orally from informants, these materials would surely be considered authentic folklore by folklorists. Since the materials are *not* in oral tradition, there are two possibilities; one can either throw out the data or throw out the theory! If we continue to cling to the oral criterion, we must reject these materials as folklore. In that event, what are the materials and who should study them? (Obviously, our position is that these materials are worthy of study no matter how they are labeled or what discipline elects to accept them for study.) The other possibility is to admit that these materials are bona fide folklore and to reject the notion that "orality" is an exclusive, definitional criterion for folklore. It is this latter position that we support.

Aside from the important theoretical implications of our materials for the future definition of "folklore," implications not likely to interest the non-folklorist, we would like to point out the intrinsic importance of the materials themselves. If old-fashioned rural folklore reflected rural American values and worldview, then it is equally likely that common urban folklore will reflect themes of importance in contemporary urban American life. Almost every major problem of urban America is touched upon in these marvelously expressive materials: racism, sex, politics, automation, alienation, women's liberation, student riots, welfare excesses, military mentality, office bureaucracy, ad infinitum. It would take an encyclopaedic sociological study to analyze exhaustively all the issues raised by the traditional materials we have assembled. We have attempted to point out some of the significant thematic content, but we readily admit that many of our observations are highly speculative. On the other hand, even if some of our comments should prove to be untenable, the basic value of the raw data will remain.

Some readers will want to see no more than the obvious humor of this material. Others will realize that the humor is a veil barely concealing an expression of most of the major problems facing contemporary American society. Many of these problems have been caused by technology. One need only think of the sense of alienation produced by filling out form applications, by receiving form-letter answers, by being identified by number rather than by name. If one can see the plight of being a small cog in a massive uncaring wheel, of being put upon by mechanistic forces of big business or government, one can readily appreciate the necessity of having urban folklore to ease the strain. Each time a personal problem is handled in an impersonal *pro forma* way—often through pat paperwork empire solutions to real-life problems— we have an occasion for folkloristic protest, an occasion not missed by the folk. In this light, it is only fitting that machines do their part in combating the states of malaise and anomie. And machines do help by aiding in the rapid and efficient transmission of urban folklore.

In defining a folk as any group that shares a common linking factor, we allow for the possibility of considering urban people as a folk bound together by the mutuality of the unhappy experiences in battling "the system," whether that system be the machinery of government or the maze where one works. If we are to work toward a more enlightened society, we need to identify the causes of social and individual ills. Urban folklore not only helps in identifying these causes, but it also provides a terribly necessary escape valve with its humor. It is in this sense that urban folklore may serve as a partial palliative or counteractant to the evils of alienation in American society.

Because the materials we present are not orally transmitted, they were difficult to collect. One cannot simply go out with a tape recorder as one would do if one were after folksongs or folktales. Individuals may remember having seen a chain letter posted on a bulletin board or a bawdy classic lying in a fellow employee's bottom drawer, but they usually cannot reproduce the item verbatim. For that reason, it has been necessary to find actual texts of all the items. It has taken us nearly ten years to assemble what we believe is a representative sampling of these long neglected forms of folklore. We feel certain that similar, if not identical, materials exist in other societies, and we hope that our efforts will encourage folklorists in other cultures to collect analogous documents. In this respect, we trust that our data will prove of interest to scholars studying other areas of the world. As more of the world becomes urbanized, there will presumably be more and more urban folklore produced. Such "folklore by facsimile" or white-collar folklore or folklore of bureaucracy represents a challenge for folklorists who have hitherto limited themselves to such conventional forms as ballads and myths. Folklore in the modern world includes urban folklore from the paperwork empire.

Work Hard and You Shall Be Rewarded

Traditional Letters

For centuries, one of the most important forms of human communication has been the letter. Letters have been so influential that often those of a famous person or the collected correspondence between two famous people are published in book form. Fictional works, including novels, have been cast in the form of a series of letters. It should come as no surprise to learn that there exists a large number of traditional letters. By "traditional letters" we mean letters that are relatively fixed in both form and content. As with all folklore, there is always the possibility, or rather probability, of variation occurring. We have numerous variants of the traditional letters presented here, but, in the interest of economy, we shall as a general rule provide only one representative text. Nevertheless, since multiple versions—usually with variations—constitute one of the best criteria to be used in determining whether a given text is folkloristic, we shall occasionally depart from this procedure by giving two or more versions of the same letter in order to demonstrate conclusively its traditionality.

One of the most common types of the traditional letter is the so-called chain letter.[1] The true chain letter is an attempt to form a human chain of communication that increases in a geometric progression as each individual recopies the single chain letter he has received and sends the five to twenty copies on to individuals he knows. Often there is an incentive, such as money, liquor, or good luck, to encourage the receiver of the letter to continue the chain. If one were to attempt to delineate the underlying structure of chain letters, one might distinguish a four-part one. First, a statement indicates that the letter is in fact a chain letter. This statement is analogous to the opening formula in fairy tales or games, for instance, "Once upon a time" or "Ready or not here I come." The second structural element is an injunction, usually directing the reader to send a certain number of copies on to friends, often stipulating a fixed period of time for compliance. The third feature consists of a description of the reward: so many recipes or blue-chip stamps or dollars will be received. Sometimes a case history of a previous "winner" is cited. The fourth and final element is a warning informing the reader what might happen if he fails to follow the instructions, thereby breaking the chain. Frequently a negative case history is presented in which a foolish individual is depicted as disregarding the injunction and losing a fortune.

In a way, one could argue that the chain letter tradition reflects one of the major patterns of achieving success in American culture. Do what you're told, conform, and there will be a payoff for you. The chain-letter instructions suggest that one must do what one is told by an external force. If one obeys, one is rewarded. If one bucks the system, one will not be rewarded and may be punished. In the case of a financial incentive, one is asked to invest a modest amount in the hope of multiplying one's investment, surely the guiding principle of capitalism. Further,

[1]For an earlier discussion, see Alan Dundes, "Chain Letter: A Folk Geometric Progression," *Northwest Folklore* 1 (1966): 14–19. For other considerations of traditional letters, see Walter Heim, *Briefe zum Himmel* (Basel: G. Krebs, 1961), or "Letters from Heaven," *Folk-Lore* 28 (1917): 318–320.

one is asked to "sell" the scheme to friends for one's own immediate gain. "Getting rich quick" is an important part of American values.

1. Think Prayer[2]

The text of our first chain letter appears to be quite fixed. Variations do occur in the names. For instance, Com. Mapak in other versions is General Napat, General Hapak, General Napok, and Gene Wapak. Even though the letters are typewritten, the variations are very much like those occurring in items transmitted orally. The overall similarity of the names plus the military title do indicate a common tradition. In terms of content, it is striking that, although the letter is ostensibly concerned with religion and prayer, the rewards are monetary. The reader is specifically told not to send money, but the case histories reveal that the good luck has a dollar value. The notion that trusting in God will result in ultimate financial success is a marvelous folk confirmation of the analysis made by economists[3] of the correlation between puritanism and capitalism.

---

[2]The title comes from one or more of the texts in our collection. In general, we have used "native" titles of texts wherever possible. However, many of the texts in our collection bore no title as such. For those texts, we improvised a title. Texts with original titles in this book include items 1, 9, 17, 20, 22, 24–31, 34–41, 43, 46, 48, 52, 54–59, 68, 73, 79–81, 85–91, 93–95. We might also note that the few texts that have been published in professional folklore journals since the completion of our study are typically not titled. For items 2, 9, 11, and 94, see Mac E. Barrick, "The Typescript Broadside," *Keystone Folklore Quarterly* 17 (1972): 27–38; for item 47, see Michael J. Preston, "Colorado State Income Tax Parody," *Western Folklore* 32 (1973): 51–52; for item 79, see Kathleen A. and Michael J. Preston, "A Note on Visual Polack Jokes," *Journal of American Folklore* 86 (1973): 175–177; for items 5, 34, 35, 39, and 71, see Michael J. Preston, "Xerox-Lore," *Keystone Folklore Quarterly* 19 (1974): 11–26.

[3]For statements on this correlation, see R. H. Tawney, *Religion and the Rise of Capitalism* (London: J. Murray, 1926), and Max Weber, *The Prot-*

"Trust in the Lord with all your might, and always acknowledge Him and He will light your way."

This prayer has been sent to you for good luck. The original copy came from the Netherlands. It has been around the world nine times. The luck has been sent to you. You are to receive good luck within four days after receiving this copy. THIS IS NO JOKE!! You will receive it in the mail. Send 20 copies of this letter to friends you think need good luck. Please do not send money. Do not keep this letter. It must leave within 96 hours after receiving it. A U.S. officer received $7,000; Don Elliott $60,000 but lost it because he broke the chain. While in the Philippines, Com. Mapak lost his life 6 days after receiving this copy. He failed to circulate the prayer. However, before his death he received $775,000 he had won. Please send 20 copies and see what happens to you on the 4th day.

2. The Fertilizer Club

This "fertilizer club" letter is, of course, a parody on the normal chain letter. It makes fun of suburban values, which delight in well-manicured lawns, but more importantly it ridicules the American toilet-training syndrome. Americans are taught to defecate in private and, unlike what occurs in many other cultures, the feces are not used in any meaningful way, for instance, as fertilizer. Evidently, the American "fear of dirt" takes priority over the normal American penchant for efficiency and utilitarianism. Incidentally, the construction of fake names for the sake of obscene puns is a widespread convention occurring both in folklore (bawdy book titles) and in literature.[4]

---

estant *Ethic and the Spirit of Capitalism* (London: G. Allen & Unwin, 1948).

[4]For examples of bawdy book titles, see Alan Dundes and Robert A. Georges, "Some Minor Genres of Obscene Folklore," *Journal of American Folklore* 75 (1962): 224; for a typical literary example of obscene name

Dear Friend:

We are sending this letter to you because you are a chain letter fan. This is a fertilizer club and will not cost you one cent to join and no dues.

Upon receipt of this letter, go to the address at the bottom of this list and shit on the lawn. You won't be the only one so don't be embarrassed.

Then make five copies of this letter, leaving off the top name and send it to five of your best friends.

You won't get any money, checks, or booze, but within one week you will have 3,216 people shitting on your lawn, if this chain is not broken.

Your reward will be next summer's greenest lawn in your block. Thank you.

1. Mr. Harry Butts   936 Corn Cob Alley
2. Mrs. Lucy Bowels   27 Bed Pan Court
3. Mrs. Smelly B. Hind   487 Diarrhea Ave.
4. Mr. G. Howie Pharts   267 Fertilizer Lane
5. Mr. I. Kant Krapp   435 Constipation Circle

3. The Spouse Exchange

In this chain-letter parody, we find a common theme in American culture, namely, the stereotype of middle-aged male impotence (signaled by "tired businessmen"), dissatisfaction with one's mate, and the common male fantasy of having an infinite number of sexual partners. It is perhaps significant that the typical American, even in fantasy, is ill-equipped for such sexuality, inasmuch as the increased sexual activity apparently causes the death of one "lucky" winner. Even in fantasy, one finds the puritan "wages of sin" motif. Note that undertakers are required in the postscript to exert quite an effort to remove the smile from the corpse. Even the outward sign of pleasure must be denied.

---

puns, see Thomas Wolfe, *Look Homeward, Angel* (New York: Charles Scribner's, 1952), p. 150.

Related to this may be the obituary custom of extolling virtues and never mentioning vices of the deceased.

Although this particular traditional letter is usually male-oriented, a version collected in 1968 is female-centered, a fact reflecting the continued rise of women's rights movements. The text is the same except that the aim is to bring relief and happiness to all ladies tired of their husbands or boyfriends and the instructions are to "bundle up your husband or boyfriend or both and send him or them to the lady at the top of the list." In the postscript, the friend receives 365 men, apparently one for each day of the year, and it takes seven undertakers thirty-six hours to get the smile off the winner's face. The greater number of undertakers and working hours suggests that women's sexual pleasure may be greater than men's!

June 20, 1957

Dear Friend:

This chain letter was started by a man like yourself in the hope it will bring relief to tired businessmen.

This does not cost you anything. Kindly send a copy of this letter to five of your friends who seem equally tired and discouraged. Bundle up your wife and send her to the man whose name appears at the top of the list and then add your name to the bottom of it.

When your name comes to the top of the list, you will receive 16,740 women. Some of them will be dandies.

You must always have faith. Do not break this chain. One man broke the chain and he got HIS OLD LADY back again.

Sincerely yours,

P.S.   At the date of this writing, a friend of mine received 556 women. They buried him yesterday. It took three undertakers 35 hours to get the smile off his face.

4. A Letter for Medgar Evers

Here we have a striking case of how such an apparently trivial folklore form as the chain letter can suddenly become a dynamic force for social protest and political action. Certainly, this example differs markedly from those chain letters in which one attempts to receive Blue Chip trading stamps or picture postcards. Here the emphasis is upon giving, not receiving, and upon providing a channel for the expression of outrage at a tragic racial assassination.

February 19, 1964

Dear ———,

I expect you dislike chain letters as much as we do, but please read on. This concerns the death of Medgar Evers in Mississippi. There are several needs that follow his tragic shooting: (1) his family needs help; (2) a large group of Americans need to express their position on this matter; (3) we need to say something effective to the governor and people of Mississippi.

An idea has been conceived by some of our friends that might accomplish these three purposes in one act. It is proposed to flood Governor Barnett's desk with envelopes containing checks for $1.00 which will automatically make him a trustee of money that he can only deliver to the Evers family. An attorney says that the checks should be made out exactly as follows: "Ross Barnett, Trustee of Memorial Fund of Family of Medgar Evers." They should be mailed to Governor Ross Barnett, State Capitol, Jackson, Mississippi. Although a new governor was inaugurated a couple of weeks ago, our checks will reach Governor Barnett and the new administration will get the message.

A number of us are receiving and transmitting this proposal as a chain of human concern. We are writing to nine other people whom we think would be interested, and if the letter goes

through five progressions in an unbroken chain, the Governor
should receive 100,000 envelopes on his desk within ten days.
We hope this will interest you!

Sincerely,

5. The President's Statue and the Promised Land

Chain letters represent only one type of traditional letter. One
of the many other types plays upon the custom of soliciting
funds for political campaigns. The following letter request for
money seems to be primarily concerned with attacking the president of the United States. The popularity of this attack on government is reflected in the fact that versions mention Roosevelt,
Eisenhower, Kennedy, Johnson, and Nixon among other presi-
dents.[5] A typical text refers to Johnson.

In one sense, it is perhaps a sad commentary on the state of
federal finances that the same parody can be so easily applied to
any of the presidential administrations since FDR. The manipu-
lation of such traditional American political symbols as George
Washington and Christopher Columbus is noteworthy. Washington survives untainted, but the context of the importance of
trade and the nature of government fiscal programs certainly
puts Columbus in a new light! The reference to Moses and the
Promised Land concerns another prominent theme in American
culture, namely, that Americans are "chosen people" blessed
with a "frontier" to be settled as part of a country that prides
itself on being the "land of opportunity."

---

[5]For earlier versions of this item, see Alan Dundes, "The President's
Statue and the Promised Land," *Journal of the Midcontinent American
Studies Association* 4 (1963): 52–55. In a version of this extremely popular
item collected in 1974 referring to Richard Nixon, there is a postscript:
"P.S. It is said that President Nixon is considering the changing of the Republican party emblem from an elephant to a condom because it stands for
inflation, protects a bunch of pricks, halts production and gives a false sense
of security while one is getting screwed!"

Dear Sir:

We have the distinction of being members of a committee to raise $50,000,000 to be used for placing a statue of Lyndon B. Johnson in the Hall of Fame in Washington, D.C.

The committee was in a quandary about selecting the proper location for the statue. It was thought unwise to place it beside that of George Washington, who never told a lie, or beside that of Franklin D. Roosevelt, who never told the truth, since Lyndon Johnson could never tell the difference.

After careful consideration, we think it should be placed next to the statue of Christopher Columbus, the greatest "New Dealer" of them all, in that he started out not knowing where he was going, and in arriving, did not know where he was, and in returning did not know where he had been, and managed to do it all on borrowed money.

The inscription on the statue will read: "I pledge allegiance to Lyndon B. Johnson and to the national debt for which he stands, one man, expendable, with graft and corruption for all."

Five thousand years ago, Moses said to the children of Israel, "Pick up your shovels, mount your asses and camels, and I will lead you to the Promised Land." Nearly five thousand years later Franklin D. Roosevelt said, "Lay down your shovels, sit on your asses, and light up a Camel, this is the Promised Land." Now Lyndon B. Johnson is stealing the shovels, kicking our asses, raising the price of Camels, and taking over the Promised Land.

If you are one of the few who has any money left after paying taxes, we will expect a generous contribution from you toward this noteworthy project.

Yours sincerely,

National Committee on the Johnson Bust

6. Dear Congressman, How Do You Stand on Whiskey?

One reason why politicians are popular subjects for ridicule is that many of them, in a concerted effort to avoid offending any of their constituents, become skilled masters of longwinded evasion. Many words are used to say very little. Hollow phrases and hackneyed clichés are intended to encourage a listener to hear what he wants to hear. The following example of fence-straddling or talking out of both sides of one's mouth may well date from Prohibition times in the 1920's in view of the concern with whiskey.

It is very difficult in Congress, as a member of Congress, to know exactly how to answer correspondence. I understand some ten or fifteen years ago, there was a Congressman in Washington who received a letter from a constituent which merely asked: "Dear Congressman, How do you stand on whiskey?"

The Congressman did not know whether the correspondent was *for* whiskey, or whether the correspondent was *against* whiskey. So he framed this letter which I believe is a very diplomatic letter.

"My Dear Friend:

I had not intended to discuss this controversial subject at this particular time. However, I want you to know that I do not shun a controversy. On the contrary, I will take a stand on any issue at any time regardless of how fraught with controversy it may be. You have asked me how I feel about whiskey; here is how I stand on this question:

If when you say whiskey, you mean the devil's brew, the poison curse, the bloody monster that defiles innocence, dethrones reason, destroys the home, creates misery and poverty, yea, literally takes the bread from the mouths of little children, if you mean the evil drink that topples the Christian man and woman from the pinnacles of righteous, gracious living into the bottomless pit of degradation and despair, shame, and helplessness and hopelessness, then certainly I am against it with all of my power.

BUT, if when you say whiskey, you mean the oil of conversation, the philosophic wine, the ale that is consumed when good fellows get together, that puts a song in their hearts and laughter on their lips and the warm glow of contentment in their eyes, if you mean Christmas cheer, if you mean the stimulating drink that puts the spring in the old gentleman's step on a frosty morning, if you mean that drink that enables a man to magnify his job and his happiness and to forget if only for a little while life's great tragedies and heartbreaks and sorrows, if you mean that drink that the sale of which pours into our treasuries untold millions of dollars, which are used to provide tender care for our little crippled children, our blind, our deaf, our dumb, our pitiful aged and infirm, to build highways, hospitals, and schools, then certainly I am in favor of it.

This is my stand, and I will not compromise. Your Congressman"

7. A Letter from an Irish Relative

To European relatives of Americans, the United States did sometimes appear to be the promised land, at least in comparison to their own countries. American relatives were expected to share the bounty with those who remained behind in the old country. This is the context of the traditional letter allegedly sent from an Irish woman in Dublin to her cousin in New York.

This traditional letter reveals much more than the relationships existing between American and Irish members of the same family. Other important themes include the Irish antagonism toward the English and the Catholic-Protestant bitterness. The repeated thanks to God for a variety of things also suggests the close connection of religious activities to Irish daily life. At the same time, it may hint of a sense of humor and realism insofar as the practical considerations come first, with God's blessing or curse requested later.

Dear Cousin Paul:

Your welcome letter received. Me and your Aunt Bridget thank you for the money you sent us. We had nine masses said for your grandmother and grandfather. God rest their souls.

You have gone to high places in America. God Bless you. I hope you'll not be putting on airs and forgetting your native land.

Your cousin, Hugh O'Toole, was hanged in Londonderry last week for killing a policeman. May God rest his soul and may God's curse be on Jimmy Callahan, the informer. May he burn in Hell, God forgive me.

Times are not as bad as they might be. The herring are back and nearly everyone is making ends meet. The price of fish is good. Thanks be to God.

We had a grand time at Pat Muldoon's wake. He was a blatherskite and it looked good to see him stretched out with his big mouth shut. He is better off dead and he'll burn till the damn place freezes over. He had too many friends among the Orangemen. God curse the lot of them. Bless your heart, I almost forgot to tell you Uncle Dinney took a pot shot at a turncoat from back of the hedge, but he had too much to drink and missed. God curse the dirty drink. I hope this letter finds you in good health and may God keep reminding you to send money.

Your cousin Biddle had a baby . . . one of them limey officers in a fancy uniform took advantage of her. He offered to marry her, but her father said "no." Better to have a bastard in the family than a bloody Englishman. God bless him and may the child never know.

Father O'Flaherty, God Bless his soul, who baptized you, is now feebleminded. He sends his blessings.

Nellie O'Malley, the brat you went to school with, has married an Englishman. They'll have no luck.

God take care of the lot of you and keep you from sudden death. Things look bright again. Every police barracks and Protestant Church in County Cork has been burned to the ground. Thanks be to God!

KEEP SENDING MONEY!

Your devoted cousin,

MAGGIE

8. Should I Tell My Bride-to-Be?

There are a number of traditional letters having to do with family problems or complaints. Not unexpectedly, the actual practice of writing letters to a newspaper columnist who offers advice to the lovelorn is parodied. Versions in the 1940's were addressed to Mr. Anthony, while 1960 texts were addressed to "Dear Abby" or Ann Landers.[6]

This traditional letter is very often localized so as to refer to particular companies, for instance, should I tell her about my cousin who works for Southern Pacific and so forth. It is noteworthy that this letter is very similar to joke structure insofar as there is a gradual build-up leading to the final punchline.

Dear Mr. Anthony,

I am a sailor in the United States Navy, and I also have a cousin who is a Republican. My father has epilepsy and my mother has syphilis, so neither of them work. They are totally dependent on my two sisters who are prostitutes in Louisville, because my only brother is serving a life term in prison for rape and murder.

I am in love with a streetwalker who operates near our base, who knows nothing of my background but says that she loves

[6]In a version of this letter published in Juliet Lowell, *Dear Mr. Congressman* (New York: Duell, Sloan, and Pearce, 1960), pp. 86–87, the cousin is a Democrat instead of a Republican. The Lowell version is dated 1947.

me. We intend to get married as soon as she settles her bigamy case, which is now in court. When I get out of the Navy we intend to move to Detroit and open up a small house.

My problem, Mr. Anthony, is this: In view of the fact that I intend to make this girl my wife and bring her into my family, should I or should I not tell her about my cousin who is a Republican?

9. To My Dear Loving Wife

While some traditional letters consist of catalogs of complaints, some are confined to a single problem. One such problem has to do with the stereotype of the oversexed husband and the undersexed wife. In this letter, the sexual incompatibility is described first from the male point of view. (The following version was collected in Downsview, Ontario, Canada, in 1969.)

To My Dear Loving Wife:

During the past year, I have attempted to seduce you 365 times. I succeeded 12 times—This averaged once every 30 days.

The following are the reasons and number of times I did not succeed:

We will wake the children	7
It's too hot	15
It's too cold	5
I'm tired	39
It's too early	23
It's too late	18
Pretending to sleep	60
Window open, neighbors will hear	9
Backache	16
Headache	10
Giggles	4
I'm too full	4
I'm hungry	8

Not in the mood	50
Baby crying	19
Watched late show	7
Watched early show	5
Not now—later	7
Mud pack	2
Grease on face	1
Reading Sunday papers	24
You're too drunk	20
Total	353

Do you think you could improve our record in the coming year?

Your loving husband

P.S. Out of the 12 successful times:
  2 times you chewed gum all the while
  3 times you watched TV all the while
  4 times you said "Hurry up and get it over with."
  2 times I had to wake you to tell you we were thru.
And one time I thought I had hurt you because I thought I felt you move.

This traditional letter contains a good deal of vital information about American sexual patterns. First, there is the male bias in the attitudes expressed. The very fact that the poor wife has to offer an excuse is already a concession to male dominance. It is also interesting that the husband is keeping score as though the particular number of instances of sexual intercourse were somehow a mark of masculinity. The husband's insistence upon seeking intercourse every single night in spite of his wife's obvious indifference suggests that marriage is like courtship or dating insofar as boys are expected to try to seduce their dates while girls are expected to resist seduction attempts—at least according to the old double-standard convention. The postscript in which the husband complains about his wife's attitudes during intercourse could easily be construed as an indictment against the husband rather than the wife. The male's lack of concern for the sexual wishes of the female is deplorable. In short, then, the letter is not so much a humorous complaint as a serious indictment of American sexual conventions, conventions that surely contribute to marital unhappiness. Although the "To My Dear Loving Wife" letter frequently occurs alone, female readers will be glad to learn that the particular version cited here was "answered" by the wife in question. The answer runs as follows:

To My Darling Husband:

I am quite aware that you attempted to seduce me 365 times last year (and your score of 12 is probably right) but being a fair and broadminded husband, I am sure you will read and consider some of my complaints also:

To begin with, those excuses I gave you were meant to inspire you, not necessarily stop you. Let's consider your first reason for my repulsing you: "We'll wake the children." My—you sure have changed. When we were single and I lived at home, we sometimes did not use the davenport because we were afraid of awakening my parents—but you didn't take "NO" for an answer then—you suggested we go for a ride or use pillows on the floor. What's the problem now? We still have a car and pillows. Second reason: "It's too cold." Remember those sub-zero nights in your convertible with cold leather seats—why you even offered to lay your coat on the seat for me, and NOW you accept "too cold or too hot" as excuses.

All the other excuses are only superficial, except the one I believe you really under-rated: "Not in the mood." During our first several years, you'd spend hours and even days just getting me "in the mood"—but now you just pat my "cheeks" and say, "How about a little tonight?" WHAT ELSE DO YOU EXPECT BUT an excuse? When we were dating, you came to see me all shined up, clean shaven—and you spent money to entertain me. Now we stay home, you seldom bathe, and expect me to accept love from a cactus bed.

Yes, honey, I think we can improve our score this year—if we both spend more time thinking about each other and what we do for each other, rather than what we can get from each other. If you will spend the time it took to prepare your report, and spend that time combing my hair—or bathing with me (like you were doing the night my parents came home early and you had to crawl out of the bathroom window), you will see that I still remember where to hide the soap and hang the wash rag.

Hopefully,

Your loving wife

The same theme is treated in non-letter form in the following calendar. In this instance, the comments give the appearance of being written by a woman rather than by a man, but it is likely that the item has a male origin in view of the expression of the undersexed female stereotype.

SUNDAY	MONDAY	TUESDAY	WEDS	THURS	FRI	SAT
1 I'M OUT OF PILLS	**2** I FORGOT TO TAKE MY PILL	**3** MY BACK HURTS	**4** I HAVE A HEADACHE	**5** IT'S 3 O'CLOCK IN THE MORNING ARE YOU OUT OF YOUR MIND?	**6** IS THAT ALL YOU EVER THINK OF?	**7** THIS IS IT MAN, GO
8 I'D LOVE TO DEAR -- BUT IT'S THAT TIME AGAIN	**9** DITTO	**10** DITTO	**11** DITTO	**12** DITTO	**13** IN BROAD DAY- <u>LIGHT</u> YOU <u>BEAST</u>	**14** I'M NOT MENTALLY IN THE MOOD
15 ALRIGHT YOU SEX FIEND	**16** IT'S TOO EARLY	**17** IT'S TOO LATE	**18** IT MIGHT AS WELL BE -- NO	**19** IN THE BATHTUB <u>YOU MUST BE</u> <u>INSANE</u>	**20** BEFORE DINNER?	**21** I WANT TO WATCH THE LATE SHOW
22 I'M TOO SLEEPY	**23** NO, YOU JUST WANT ME FOR MY BODY	**24** IF YOU INSIST, BUT WHAT IS A MATINEE?	**25** DIDN'T I TELL YOU I'M STAYING AT MOTHERS TONIGHT?	**26** WHAT DO YOU MEAN WHAT AM I SAVING IT FOR -- DON'T TALK RACEY	**27** YOU WANT ME TO WHAT?	**28** ALRIGHT, BUT HURRY UP ITS MORNING
29 NO, AND DON'T GIVE ME THAT - I'M NOT A WOMAN ---	**30** WITH THE LIGHTS ON -- WHAT DO YOU THINK I --	**31** NO, NO, NO, WHAT'S A SWAP CLUB?	"NO" IS A TWO LETTER WORD		BETTER LUCK NEXT MONTH ---- TIGER	

10. Full of Corn

An unusual letter of complaint makes use of pseudo-rural humor with a number of puns, corny puns at that, and exaggeration through understatement. This type of humor was extremely popular in nineteenth-century America, and it continues to delight people in rural areas.[7] Sophisticated urbanites may groan at some of the forced word play, but no doubt they will also appreciate the remarkable ingenuity of the letter writer.

Dear you,

As I have time because I ain't busy, I thought I would write you the up-to-date news about six months old. We are both well as can be expected for the condition we are in. We ain't sick, just don't feel good. I am feeling fine but the neighbor died. Hope you are feeling the same.

I suppose you are anxious to hear about our moving. We never started to move until we left. We never turned off until we came to the crossroad that went there. It didn't take us any longer than from the time we started until we arrived. The trip was the best part of all. If you ever come over here, don't miss that. No one expected to see us until we arrived and most of the people we were acquainted with we know. The people we don't know seem like strangers. We still live in the same place we moved to last, which is beside our nearest neighbors across the road from the other side. Jim thinks we will stay here until we move or go somewhere else.

We are very busy farming three cows. We are going to sell one because we can't milk him. Eggs are a good price. That is

[7]For discussion of American humor, see Constance Rourke, *American Humor* (New York: Harcourt, Brace, 1931), Walter Blair, *Native American Humor (1800–1900)* (New York: American Book Co., 1937), and Richard Dorson, *American Folklore* (Chicago: University of Chicago Press, 1959), pp. 39–73.

the reason they are so high. I sure hope we get a lot of them. We just bought 25 roosters and an old hen. Some of the ground is so poor you can't raise an umbrella on it, but we have a fine crop of potatoes. Some the size of peas and then a lot of little ones. We also have a fine crop of corn. I think we will make about five gallons to the acre. Some worms got in our corn last year, but we fished them out and drank it anyway. Our romance started on a gallon of corn and ended with a full crib.

Our dog died last week. Jim said he swallowed a tape line and died by the inch. Mom said he went up the back alley and died by the yard. Sis said he crawled up under the bed and died by the foot.

My mother-in-law is sick and at death's door. Sure hope the doctor can pull her through. Jane fell off the back porch and bruised her somewhat, and skinned her elsewhere. Alice has the mumps and is having a swell time.

I have a photographic memory for news; I don't think anything will develop.

Every time Jim gets sick, he starts feeling bad; the doctor gave him some medicine and said if he gets better it might help him, and if he didn't get worse he would probably stay the same. I would have sent the $5 I owe you, but I already had this letter sealed before I thought about it. I am sending you an overcoat; I cut the buttons off so it wouldn't be so heavy—you will find them in the left-hand pocket. We are out of jelly, so I am sending Jim downtown for some of that traffic jam.

I am putting your address on the inside of the envelope so it won't rub off. I must close now . . . if you don't get to read this let me know and I will mail it to you. If you can't read my writing, make a copy of it and read your own.

Be sure and write—even if it's nothing but a check.

Love,

Me again

11. A Strange Blend of Coffee

Another example of what many might term unsophisticated humor involves the use of dialect, in this case a fake German or German-American dialect. The premise concerns receipt of a shipment of coffee in Germany from an American company. Apparently, the coffee bags were visited during the voyage by rats who proceeded to nest in the coffee. The shipper discovers the damage but simply sews up the bags and dispatches the shipment to its destination. The German firm then sends the following letter.

There are many interesting aspects of this letter. First, the oral dialect humor is carried over into written tradition. Second, international business etiquette, in which normal outrage must be politely expressed, is ridiculed. But perhaps the most interesting feature of all is the use of rat feces in connection with Germans. The American stereotype of the German national character depicts the German as neat, clean, militaristic, and well organized. In view of this stereotype, the German importer's receipt of coffee mixed with rat feces is particularly striking. Possibly, the letter reflects the anti-German sentiments remaining from the First and Second World Wars. In American folk speech, there are several idioms involving feces. Asking or forcing an opponent to "eat shit" is to humiliate him. Similarly, no one likes to "take shit from anyone." These metaphors are particularly common in army slang; for instance, an officer who insists upon the letter of the law in discipline or regulations is termed "chickenshit." Since the letter itself reminds the reader that it comes from the American zone in occupied Germany, it is certainly possible that the mixture of feces and food is intended to humiliate the former enemy.

136 Wilhelm Strasse
Hamburg, Germany
American Zone

Andrews Coffee Company
435 West 139th Street
New York, New York, U.S.A.

Schentlemens:

Der last two schippmundts of koffee ve gott from you vas mitt ratt schidt germixed. Der koffee may be gootenuff, but der ratt schidt schpoils der trade ve got.

Ve did not see der ratt schidt in der samples vich you sendt befor to us. It iss taken too much time to pik der ratt schidt from der koffee oudt.

Ve order from you der kleen koffee, und you shipt germixed mitt ratt schidt yet. Idt is a mishtake Yes, No?

Ve like you to schipp der koffee in vun sack und der ratt schidt in vun odder sack, den ve germix to zoot our kustomer.

Vont you bleeze wride if ve should schipp back der schidt und keep der koffee, or keep der schidt und schipp back der koffee. Or do you vant ve should schipp bak der hole schidten vorks.

Ve vant to do vat iss ridt in dis madder, but ve do not lik dis dam ratt schidten businesses.

Mitt Mutsch Respecht,

Hans Bruder
Importer

Pee Ess—Iss der price der same as mittout, as mitt der ratt schidt?

12. The Bill Payer's Complaint

One of the most popular complaints in traditional letters has to do with requests for money. In such letters, the angry writer protests against paying a bill, usually mentioning all his other financial obligations and personal mishaps. Here is a specimen.

Dear Sir:

In reply to your request to send a check, I wish to inform you that the present condition of my bank account makes it almost impossible. My shattered financial condition is due to Federal Laws, State Laws, County Laws, Brothers-in-Laws, Sisters-in-Laws and Outlaws.

Through these laws, I am compelled to pay a business tax, amusement tax, head tax, school tax, gas tax, light tax, water tax, sales tax, liquor tax, income tax, furniture tax and excise tax. I am required to get a business license, car license, operator's license, truck license, not to mention a marriage license and dog license.

I am also required to contribute to every society and organization which the genius of man is capable of bringing to life; to women's relief, the unemployed relief and the gold digger's relief. Also to every hospital and charitable institution in the city, including the Salvation Army, Community Chest, Red Cross, Purple Cross, Double Cross, Boy Scouts, Cub Scouts, Y.M.C.A., Y.W.C.A., as well as Wayward Stations for Wayward Girls, Boy's Ranch and Boy's Town.

For my own safety, I am required to carry health insurance, life insurance, fire insurance, unemployment insurance, compensation insurance and old-age insurance.

My business is so governed that it is no easy matter to find out who owns it. I am expected, inspected, required, summoned, fined, commanded and compelled, until I provide an inexhaustible supply of money for every known need, desire or hope of the human race.

Simply because I refuse to donate to something or other, I am boycotted, talked about, lied about, held up, held down and robbed until I am almost ruined.[8]

---

[8]The one version of this traditional item that we were able to find in print ends as follows: "All I know is that I am supposed to be an inexhaustible supply of money for every human need, desire or hope of the human race,

I can tell you honestly that except for a miracle that happened I could not enclose this check. The wolf that comes to many doors nowadays just had pups in my kitchen. I sold them, and here is the money.

Yours very truly,

P.S. Regards to all the boys

13. The Debtor's Letter

A classic traditional letter is one ostensibly written to a retail creditor. This particular letter, which we have termed "the debtor letter," is an eloquent protest against the evils of buying on the installment plan. An inherent danger in the plan is, of course, that the object purchased may be irreparably damaged or destroyed long before the purchaser has finished making all the payments for it. Installment credit and collection agencies are now very much a part of American life, which may explain the continued popularity of such an extended folk commentary upon this institution.

Because this specimen is such a venerable example of a traditional American letter, we shall present two versions, one dating from 1943 and the other from 1960. If the dates mentioned in the body of the letter mean anything at all, the debtor letter is probably much older than 1943. Although the letter demonstrates remarkable stability over time, one finds numerous variations in detail—as one would expect to find in any authentic item of folklore.

---

and because I will not sell all I have and go out and beg, borrow or steal money to give away I have been cussed, discussed, boycotted, talked to, talked about, lied to, lied about, held up, robbed and nearly ruined, and the only reason I am clinging to life is to see what in h——l is coming off next." See "So Say We: All of Us!" *The Competitor* 1, no. 3 (March 1920): 79.

Pine Bluff, Ca.
Sept. 4, 1943

Bakerfield Hardware Co.
Bakerfield, Ca.

Gentlemen,

Your letter to hand this morning in an open envelope with a one cent stamp on it and it would have given me and the boys at the Post Office much pleasure and amusement had not the melancholy reflection come with it, that there are shysters in this country who have the guts to dun an American citizen with an open letter and a one cent stamp on it.

You speak of honor. If you are an honorable credit manager you know whereof I speak when I say that if there were an honorable credit manager in the world, he would go around crying, "Hardware for sale." You said you thought the bill could have been paid long ago and could not understand why it had not. I will enlighten you.

In 1907 I bought a saw mill on credit, in 1908 an ox team, a timber cart, two texas ponies, a $50.00 Colt revolver, two fine razorback hogs, a set of books, all on the unchristly installment plan. In 1909 the mill burned down and didn't leave me a damn thing, one of my ponies died and I loaned the other to a son-of-a-bitch peddler that starved him to death, then I joined the Church, the populist party and the farmers alliance, and was beaten for constable by one vote. In 1910 my father died and my brother was lynched for horse stealing. A railroad man knocked up my sister and the dirty bastard ran away, and I had to pay $88.00 doctor's bill to keep the little bastard from being a relative of mine. In 1911 my boy got the mumps and they went down on him and the doctor had to castrate him to save his life. Later I went fishing and the boat upturned and I lost the biggest catfish I ever saw, and two of my boys drowned (neither being the one that was castrated).

In 1912 I burned out again. Then I took to drinking and didn't stop until all I had was a stricture and a Waterbury watch. For some time I was kept busy between winding my watch and running to piss. In 1915 my wife ran away with a heavy hung nigger, and he left me with a pair of nine months old twins for souvenirs. Then I married the hired girl to keep down expenses, but I had trouble getting her to go off. I went to the doctor and he advised me to create some excitement about the time I thought she was ready. That night I took my shotgun to bed with me and just when I thought she was ready, I stuck the gun out the window and fired. My wife shit in bed. I bit the nipple off her tit, ruptured myself, and I shot the best damned cow I ever had.

The next year I took heart again and bought a manure spreader, a Deering binder, and a threshing machine, all on credit again, when a cyclone came and blew everything I had into the next county. Then my wife caught the clap from a traveling salesman and my son wiped his ass on a corn cob that had rat poison on it and someone nutted my bull.

Nothing surprised me more than when you said you could cause me trouble. Now if you can see when I missed any trouble, for Christ sake dig in. I tell you that getting money out of me would be like trying to poke butter up a wildcat's ass with a red-hot poker. I swear to God mister, that if fat geese were selling for 1¢ a piece, I couldn't kiss a humming bird's ass.

If you bastards are as small in stature as you are in principle, you could stand flat-footed and kiss a chicken's ass without bending your knees.

I am praying for a storm of skunk shit to fall and I hope that the storm centers around that particular bunch of bastards who get their mail at the Bakerfield Post Office.

Yours very truly,

Silas Nutterbuster

A second version is as follows:

Blossom Gulch, Arkansaw
December 10, 1960

The Bakerfield Company
Saint Louis, Missouri

Your super heated letter arrived here this morning in an open envelope, with a one cent stamp on it, and should have given me and the boys much pleasure and amusement, had not the melancholy reflection come with it that there were shysters in this country, who have the guts to dun an American citizen with an open letter, with a one-cent stamp on it.

You speak of honor—you call yourself a credit manager, and you said you thought the bill could have been paid a long time ago, and you couldn't understand why it wasn't. Well I'll enlighten you a bit.

In 1907 I bought a saw mill on credit. In 1908 an ox cart, two ponies, a breech-loading Winchester shot-gun, a twenty-five dollar revolver and two fine razor-back hogs, all on that damn installment plan.

In 1909, the mill burned down and didn't leave a damn thing. One of my ponies died and I loaned the other to an inebriated circumsized son-of-a-bitch of a new [Jew] peddler and he starved it to death, so I joined the church.

In 1910 my father died, and my brother was lynched for horse stealing. A railroader knocked my daughter up and I had to pay $88.00 to a doctor to keep the little bastard from becoming a relative of mine. In 1911 my boy got the mumps and they went down on him so that they had to castrate him to save his life. Later I went fishing and the boat turned over with me and I lost the biggest catfish I ever saw, and two of my boys drowned, neither being the castrated one.

In 1915 my wife ran away with a blue-gum nigger, and left me with a pair of cross-eyed twins for a souvenir. Then I married the hired girl to keep expenses down, but had trouble getting her to go off. I went to the doctor and he advised me to create some excitement about the time she was ready. That night I stuck the

shot-gun out the window and fired. My wife shit the bed, I ruptured myself, and shot the best damn cow I had.

In 1931, I again burned out and took to drinking. I didn't stop
until all I had left was a Waterbury watch and a stricture. Then
for some time I was kept busy winding my watch and running
to piss. The next year I took heart again and purchased a manure
spreader, a Deering binder and a threshing machine, all on
credit, and then came the cyclone and blew everything into the
next county. My wife caught the clap from a traveling salesman,
my boy wiped his ass on a corncob that had rat poison on it, and
some bastard nutted the best bull I had.

Nothing surprised me more than when you said you could
cause me trouble. Now if you see anything that I have missed,
then for Christ sake dig in. I am so broke that if wild geese were
selling for 10¢ a dozen, I couldn't afford to kiss a humming
bird's ass. Trying to get money out of me would be like trying
to pour hot butter up a wild-cat's ass with a straw.⁹ Now if you
are as small in stature as you are in principle, you could stand
flat-footed and kiss a gnat's ass without bending your knees. I am
praying for a storm of skunk piss and I hope it centers over that
particular part of Saint Louis where you bastards get your mail.

                                                          RED HETZEL

P.S. If I wasn't the Pastor of our little town, I'd really tell you
what I think.

A comparison of the two versions (and of other versions not
presented here) reveals that the formulas in the letter are rela-

⁹Here is an obvious instance of variation. In the first version, butter is
manipulated with a red-hot poker. In another version collected in 1960, the
letter ends as follows: "Now at the present time you say you could cause
me trouble, but if it would cost a nickel to take a shit, I'd have to vomit.
Trying to get money out of me now would be like trying to poke horse shit
up a wildcat's ass with a toothpick, but mister you sure are welcome to try."
In a version collected in 1969, the material placed is once again butter, but
the tool in question is a "hot awl."

tively stable. Among the many repeated themes in the letter is the one of male impotence. The man's wife runs away with another man, he has trouble in satisfying his second wife, and both his son and prize bull are castrated. Aggravating the situation is the fact that the letter writer's women are victimized by other males. The daughter becomes pregnant and requires an abortion, the first wife runs off with a Negro who according to the white stereotype offers greater sexuality, and the second wife proves unfaithful inasmuch as she catches the "clap" from a traveling salesman. All this confirms the notion that misfortune is frequently perceived in purely sexual terms or at least sexuality provides a common metaphor for catastrophe.

14. The Temperance Recruiter

A most curious traditional letter refers to the once widespread temperance movement in the United States. This letter is nearly unique among traditional letters insofar as it directly involves the reader of the letter. The letter is similar to a "catch tale" or catch riddle to the extent that the reader is "caught" at the end. (The purpose of catch tales or catch riddles is to "catch" the dupe-listener. For instance, one child asks another, "Did you get the letter I sent you?" When the second child says, "No," the first replies, "Well that's because I forgot to *stamp* it," whereupon he "stamps" the victim's foot with his own.)

Kansas City, Mo.
Sept. 14, 1966

Dear Friend,

Perhaps you've heard of me and about my state-wide campaign in the cause of temperance. Each year, for the past fourteen years, I have made a tour of the state of Missouri and delivered a series of lectures on the evils of drinking.

On these tours I have been accompanied by my young friend

and assistant, Herman Forsythe. Herman was a pathetic case—a young man of good family and excellent background, whose life was ruined because of excessive indulgence in whiskey, gin, and rum. How much better it would have been had he turned to the Lord.

Herman would appear with me at my lectures and sit on the platform drooling at the mouth and staring at the audience, through bleary bloodshot eyes, while I would point him out as an example of what drink would do.

Last spring, unfortunately, poor Herman died. A mutual friend has given me your name and I wonder if you would care to accompany me on my winter tour and take poor Herman's place.

> Yours in Faith
> (Signed) Alvin B. Smith
> THE REV. ALVIN B. SMITH
> Temperance Society
> Kansas City, Missouri

15. Thank You from the Old Folks Home

A traditional letter that loses most, if not all, of its impact if it is not handwritten is the thank-you letter from a resident in a home for the aged. For maximum shock value, it is essential that the letter be written in an old-fashioned, shaky hand. The letter reveals one of the dominant problems of American society, namely, what is to be done with/for the elderly? With American society's insistence upon forced retirement on reaching a certain age and with the nature of households built around nuclear families there seems to be no place for the aged. Grandparents are shunted off to retirement homes whose meager facilities are partly glossed over by such glamorous names as "Happy Acres." As a result, the aged in America may end their lives not with their families but with strangers.

In this letter, we discover two ladies and the friction that exists between them over minor material objects. The fact that so common an item as a radio is not available (in some versions the object is a hair dryer) indicates the material as well as the spiritual poverty of the retirement-home milieu. Another feature of this traditional letter is the stereotype of innocence, or at least sexlessness, of old people, especially old women. Americans seem to believe that sexuality is reserved for the middle years. Young children and the elderly are (wrongly) presumed to be disinterested in sexual activities and sexual language. In reality, neither the very young nor the very old are unaware of sexuality. The letter certainly suggests this by the contrast between the seeming religious innocence of the letter writer and her final use of the vernacular.

Dear Sir,

I am sure the Wilton Retirement Home has thanked you and the many others who made gifts to the Home that have brought pleasure and comfort to us residents.

But I wish to thank you personally from the bottom of my heart because I am the recipient of the little portable radio which you gave me. I listen to it constantly when I am awake.

It has been so much company for me I have wanted a radio of my very own ever since I came to the home to live. We have nice accommodations here and they take very good care of us. There are two of us in each room. My room mate is Blanche Ginling. She is 87 & I am 83.

Blanche has had a radio of her own ever

since she came here, two years ago. she kept it so low I could never hear the programs. When I would ask her to turn it up so I could hear the programs too, she wouldn't do it. Bless her, she is a sweet old soul and I suppose she just can't help being that way.

Last week she dropped her radio and it broke into many pieces and cannot be repaired. Last night I was listening to the early evening service of the First Methodist Church and those beautiful old hymns I love so much Blanche asked me to turn the radio up higher so she could hear it too, so naturally I told her to go fuck herself.

Again thank you
am
Marjorie Winters

It is noteworthy that American humor makes use of an unexpected obscenity as the punchline. The same technique as that employed in the Old Folks Home letter is found in any one of the numerous folk poems about the bird perching on the window sill. Here we have not only obscenity, but a strange passion for violence. The American pleasure in destroying nature has only recently been investigated by ecology-oriented groups. The bird poem is as follows:

> A robin perched upon my sill
> and started in to sing.
> The beauty of his lovely voice
> of happiness did bring.
>
> He stayed awhile and sang no more
> and during this sudden lull,
> I softly closed the window
> and broke his fucking skull!

In another version, the innocence of childhood heightens the contrast.

> Good Morning
>
> By Donna Smith
> Age 8
>
> The sun was shining brightly
> And I could hardly wait
> To ponder at my window
> And gaze at my estate.
>
> The breeze was blowing briskly
> It made the flowers sway
> The garden was enchanting
> On this inspiring day.
>
> My eyes fell on a little bird
> With a beautiful yellow bill
> I beckoned him to come and light
> Upon my window sill.

I smiled at him cheerfully
And gave him a crust of bread
Then I quickly closed the window
And smashed his fucking head.

Both these versions, incidentally, are transmitted by office copier.

16. Pardon This Jerky Writing

A traditional letter depending even more upon being handwritten is the following. It is difficult to imagine how this particular text could have any impact in typewritten or printed form. On the other hand, it is reproducible by any office copier, and it frequently circulates by this means. As noted previously, a common technique is to parody letters to popular advice columnists, such as Ann Landers. Once again we find the popular theme of the sexually aggressive male taking advantage of a victimized female.

Dear Ann Landers:

After 5 years of marriage I am firmly convinced I am married to a sex maniac.

My problem is this. He insists on making love to me at all hours of the day, regardless of what I am doing -- the dishes, making the bed, or tending the children -- What do you suggest?

Sincerely yours,
Matilda Anderson

P.S. Please pardon this jerky writing.

17. Grammar as Wrote

So much communication depends upon letter-writing skills that it is essential that schoolchildren be exposed to this form early in their education. Children are taught the fundamentals of letter writing just as they are taught a whole host of compositional principles. As a matter of fact, the very process of teaching composition is itself the subject of a traditional letter. Admittedly, this traditional letter seems to be designed as a teaching aid.[10] Its titles include "Grammar as Wrote" and "Rools of Grammore."

Dear Sir; you never past me in grammar because you was prejudice but I got this here athaletic scholarship any way. Well, the other day I finely get to writing the rule's down so I can always study it if they ever slip my mind.
1. Each pronoun agrees with their antecedent.
2. Just between you and I, case is important.
3. Verbs has to agree with their subjects.
4. Watch out for irregular verbs which has crope into our language.
5. Don't use no double negatives.
6. A writer mustn't shift your point of view.
7. When dangling, don't use participles.
8. Join clauses good, like a conjunction should.
9. Don't write a run-on sentence you got to punctuate it.
10. About sentence fragments.
11. In letters themes reports articles and stuff like that we use commas to keep a string of items apart.
12. Don't use commas, which aren't necessary.
13. Its important to use apostrophe's right.
14. Don't abbrev.
15. Check to see if you any words out.

[10]The source of this traditional communication seems to be George W. Feinstein, "Letters from a Triple-Threat Grammarian," *College English* 21 (1959–1960): 408. However, his twenty rules have become fifteen.

18. The College Girl's Letter Home

Just as some of the problems of grammar school are displayed in a traditional letter, one should not be surprised to discover that some of the worries of college life also find expression in a traditional letter. In the following text collected in 1968, we find an itemized list of almost all the fears middle-class white parents have about their daughters who go off to college. Here we see how well folklore encapsulates the culture that surrounds it. If one were to ask a parent what the principal worries were about a daughter at college, it is unlikely that he would obtain such a concise and complete catalog as the one found in this letter. Note also that the girl is well aware of parental anxieties, and she skillfully plays upon these anxieties and upon the generation gap for her own advantage.

Dear Mother and Dad:
It has been three months since I left for college. I have been remiss in writing and I am very sorry for my thoughtlessness in not having written before. I will bring you up to date now, but before you read on, please sit down. You are not to read any further unless you are sitting down, okay?
Well then, I am getting along pretty well now. The skull fracture and the concussion I got when I jumped out of the window of my dormitory when it caught fire shortly after my arrival are pretty well healed by now. I only spent two weeks in the hospital and now I can see almost normally and only get those headaches once a day.
Fortunately, the fire in the dormitory and my jump was witnessed by an attendant at the gas station near the dorm, and he was the one who called the Fire Dept. and the ambulance. He also visited me at the hospital and since I had nowhere to live because of the burnt out dormitory, he was kind enough to invite me to share his apartment with him. It's really a basement room,

but it's kind of cute. He is a very fine boy and we have fallen deeply in love and are planning to get married. We haven't set the exact date yet, but it will be before my pregnancy begins to show.

Yes, mother and dad, I am pregnant. I know how very much you are looking forward to being grandparents and I know you will welcome the baby and give it the same love and devotion and tender care you gave me when I was a child. The reason for the delay in our marriage is that my boyfriend has some minor infection which prevents us from passing our premarital blood tests and I carelessly caught it from him. This will soon clear up with the penicillin injections I am now taking daily.

I know you will welcome him into the family with open arms. He is kind and although not well educated, he is ambitious. Although he is of a different race and religion than ours, I know that your oft-expressed tolerance will not permit you to be bothered by the fact that his skin color is somewhat darker than ours. I am sure you will love him as I do. His family background is good too, for I am told his father is an important gunbearer in the village in Africa from which he comes.

Now that I have brought you up to date, I want to tell you there was no dormitory fire; I did not have a concussion or a skull fracture; I was not in the hospital; I am not pregnant; I am not engaged. I do not have syphillis, and there is no Negro in my life. However, I am getting a D in Sociology and an F in science; and I wanted you to see these marks in the proper perspective.

Your loving daughter,

19. Letter to a Buddy in the Service

If a college girl's letter home can cause anguish, equally painful can be those written from home. Men in the armed forces depend heavily upon such letters, which they frequently regard as the major link with "life on the outside," that is, civilian life.

One type of letter especially dreaded is the "Dear John" letter, as it is commonly referred to. In a "Dear John" letter, the serviceman's sweetheart writes to tell him that she is no longer waiting for him to return and that she has found someone else.

In the following letter ostensibly written by a serviceman's close friend, we find the theme of infidelity confirming the serviceman's worst fears. At least a "Dear John" letter, painful though it may be, is direct and honest. This letter written by a pal is cruel, the parodistic element notwithstanding.

Dear Buddy:

Nothing much doing back here. I sure do envy you out there in Viet Nam, right in the thick of things. Bet you never have a dull moment.

I was over to see your wife last night and read all your letters. They were a bit mushy, but I don't blame you. Frances is a swell girl, wonderful figure, good looks and personality. The guys still whistle at her when she walks down the street.

Your brother-in-law Smedley dropped in—he was wearing the brown suit you bought just before you left. Frances gave it to him as she thought it would be out of style when you get back. Several other couples came in and we killed two cases of beer. We wanted to chip in for it, but Fran wouldn't let us. She said you sent $10.00 extra for her to spend as she wished. One of the guys is buying your golf clubs, too. He paid $25.00 for them and will pick them up tomorrow. That is more than she got for your movie camera and projector.

Frances was the life of the party. I thought she would be a little shaken up after the accident last week with your Chevy but you'd never have known she had been in a head-on collision and smashed your car to bits. The other driver is still in the hospital and threatens to sue; too bad Fran forgot to pay the insurance—but, funny thing, she isn't a bit worried. We all admire her courage and nonchalance and especially her willingness to mortgage the house to pay the bill. Good thing you gave her the power of attorney before you left.

Well, to get back to the party—you should have seen Fran do an imitation of "Gypsy Rose." She has the figure, and was still going strong when we said goodnight to her and Claude. Guess you know Claude is rooming at the house. It is close to his work and he saves a lot of gas and lunches, and can stay in bed a little longer in the mornings.

Nothing much new with me, except my wife got another raise. $100 a week now—so we do O.K. with the $115 I get at the office. It is getting late, so I will stop. I can see through my window across the street to your front porch. Frances and Claude are having a little nite cap. He is wearing your smoking jacket, the yellow one you liked so well.

Well, Buddy, I sure wish I could be over there with you. LUCKY GUY! Give those Commies "HELL."

Your Pal,

Eddie

20. The Twelve Days of Christmas

Parody can only be effective if the object being parodied is already well known to the audience. Our final example of a traditional letter consists of a series or sequence of letters based upon the familiar Christmas carol or folktale "The Twelve Days of Christmas."[11] The standard poetic device of incremental repetition serves equally well in a "thank you" letter format. In this literal enactment of gift giving, the innocence of Christmas is replaced by sex, sadism, and violence, which may well be a more realistic reflection of current tendencies in American society.

---

[11]For references, see Aarne-Thompson tale type 2010A, The Twelve Days (Gifts) of Christmas, in Stith Thompson, *The Types of the Folktale*, 2d rev. ed. (Helsinki: Academia Scientiarum Fennica, 1961).

Miss Agnes McHolstein
69 Copeland Drive
New Canaan, Connecticut
October 14, 1972

Dearest Hunter:
   I went to the door today and the postman delivered a partridge in a pear tree. What a thoroughly delightful gift. I couldn't have been more surprised.

With deepest love & devotion,

Agnes

Miss Agnes McHolstein
69 Copeland Drive
New Canaan, Connecticut
October 15, 1972

Dearest Hunter:
   Today the postman brought your very sweet gift. Just imagine two turtle doves. I'm just delighted at your very thoughtful gift. They are just adorable.

All my love,

Agnes

Miss Agnes McHolstein
69 Copeland Drive
New Canaan, Connecticut
October 16, 1972

Dear Hunter:
   Aren't you the extravagant one. Now I really must protest. I don't deserve such generosity, three French hens. They are just darling, but I must insist, you've been too kind.

Love,

Agnes

Miss Agnes McHolstein
69 Copeland Drive
New Canaan, Connecticut
October 17, 1972

Dear Hunter:

Today the postman delivered four calling birds. Now really, they are beautiful but don't you think enough is enough. You're being too romantic.

Affectionately,

Agnes

Miss Agnes McHolstein
69 Copeland Drive
New Canaan, Connecticut
October 18, 1972

Dearest Hunter:

What a surprise. Today the postman delivered five golden rings, one for every finger. You're just impossible, but I love it. Frankly, all those birds squeaking were beginning to get on my nerves.

All my love,

Agnes

Miss Agnes McHolstein
69 Copeland Drive
New Canaan, Connecticut
October 19, 1972

Dear Hunter:

When I opened the door there were actually six geese a laying on my front steps. So you're back to the birds again, huh? Those geese are huge. Where will I ever keep them? The neighbors are complaining and I can't sleep through the racket.

Please stop.

Cordially,

Agnes

Miss Agnes McHolstein
69 Copeland Drive
New Canaan, Connecticut
October 20, 1972

Hunter:
  What's with you and those fucking birds??? Seven swans a swimming. What kind of God-damned joke is this? There's bird shit all over the house and I'm a nervous wreck, it's not funny. So stop with those fucking birds.

Sincerely,

Agnes

Miss Agnes McHolstein
69 Copeland Drive
New Canaan, Connecticut
October 21, 1972

OK Buster:
  I think I prefer the birds. What the hell am I going to do with eight maids a milking? It's not enough with all those birds and eight maids a milking, but they had to bring their God-damned cows. There is shit all over the lawn and I can't move in my own house. Just lay off me, smartass.

Agnes

Miss Agnes McHolstein
69 Copeland Drive
New Canaan, Connecticut
October 22, 1972

Hey Shithead:
  What are you? Some kind of sadist? Now there's nine pipers playing. And Christ, do they play. They've never stopped chasing those maids since they got here yesterday morning. The cows are getting upset and they're stepping all over those screeching

birds. What am I going to do? The neighbors have started a petition to evict me.

You'll get yours,

Agnes

Miss Agnes McHolstein
69 Copeland Drive
New Canaan, Connecticut
October 23, 1972

You rotten prick:

Now there's ten ladies dancing. I don't know why I call those sluts ladies. They've been balling those pipers all night long. Now the cows can't sleep and they've got the diarrhea. My living room is a river of shit. The Commissioner of Buildings has subpoenaed me to give cause why the building shouldn't be condemned.

I'm siccing the police on you.

One who means it

Miss Agnes McHolstein
69 Copeland Drive
New Canaan, Connecticut
October 24, 1972

Listen fuckhead:

What's with the 11 lords a leaping on those maids and ladies? Some of those broads will never walk again. Those pipers ran through the maids and have been committing sodomy with the cows. All 23 of the birds are dead. They've been trampled to death in the orgy. I hope you're satisfied, you rotten vicious swine.

Your sworn enemy,

Agnes

Law Offices
Badger, Bender and Cahole
303 Knave Street
Hartford, Connecticut
October 25, 1972

Dear Sir:

This is to acknowledge your latest gift of the 12 fiddlers fiddling which you have seen fit to inflict on our client, Miss Agnes McHolstein. The destruction, of course, was total. All correspondence should come to our attention. If you should attempt to reach Miss Agnes McHolstein at Happy Dale Sanitorium, the attendants have instructions to shoot you on sight. With this letter, please find a warrant for your arrest.

Cordially,

Badger, Bender and Cahole

Definitions and Principles

Among the most popular forms of urban folklore circulated in offices is the list of humorous definitions, purported typologies, or pseudo-scientific laws. Every folk group—be it an occupational group or an office unit—has its own jargon. Frequently, a given group will appropriate the "definitions" format and adapt it to its own esoteric needs. On the other hand, a large number of traditional definitions continues to be popular. Of special interest to the social scientist is the thematic content of the various definitions. It is surely a commentary upon American society that so many of the folk definitions concern sexuality.

It should also be noted that the very attempt to define subjective states in objective terms or to formulate pretentious "laws" of human weaknesses is itself a significant reflection of American ideology. Americans claim to prefer objectivity, precision, and rational order. Yet they constantly seek outlets for subjectivity, sloppiness, and irrational behavior. This search is unquestionably one of the crucial functions of this type of urban folklore. It acts as a cultural safety valve for the pressures that build up from the long puritanical denial of the body and from the fanatic worship of science.

21. Modern Definitions

There are numerous lists of definitions. Many of these definitions find their way into anthologies of humor although not always in uncensored form. The following set of "modern definitions" dates from the 1930's and early 1940's.[1]

Brassiere: A device that makes mountains out of mole hills and vice-versa.

Pajamas: Item of clothing taken on a honeymoon in case of fire.

Papoose: Consolation prize for taking a chance on an Indian blanket.

Virginity: A bubble on the stream of life that vanishes with the first prick.

Prostitute: A busy-body.

Mistress: Something between a mister and a mattress.

Minute-man: A fellow who double parks in front of a whore-house with his engine running.

Rhumba: An asset to good music.

Adultery: Two wrong people doing the right thing.

Vice: Anything you enjoy that is bad for you.

Conscience: That little thing that feels bad when you are feeling good.

Mother's Day: Nine months after father's day.

Kiss: Uptown shopping for downtown business.

Alimony: The screwing you get for the screwing you got.

Wife: A gadget you screw on the bed to get the housework done.

[1]For further discussion of "definitions," see Alan Dundes and Robert A. Georges, "Some Minor Genres of Obscene Folklore," *Journal of American Folklore* 75 (1962): 223–224.

22. A Glossary of Naval Terms

The following "glossary of Naval terms" dating from the early 1940's illustrates an occupational localization of the definition format. Many business offices have evolved strikingly similar definitions for the conventional language of transmittal slips.

"Take necessary action" . . . It's your headache now.

"We should confer" . . . Send your yeoman over to see mine.

"Forwarded" . . . Pigeon-holed in a more ornate office.

"A growing body of naval opinion" . . . Two brass hats have agreed.

"Take immediate action" . . . Do something in a hurry before we both catch hell.

"For your information" . . . Let's both forget it.

"Your observations are desired" . . . Do the dirty work so I can write "forwarded."

"Your department is negligent" . . . I have just been given hell.

"You are to be commended" . . . There is a particularly dirty job coming in the next routing.

"Naval tradition demands" . . . I have just been talking to an old chief.

"Give this your immediate action" . . . For God's sake find the papers.

"You will show him every courtesy" . . . His uncle is an admiral.

"The inspection party has departed" . . . How about a binge tonight?

23. Office Definitions

This list of office definitions collected at a Douglas Aircraft plant in Los Angeles in 1964 illustrates the continuity of this form of office folklore. Most of the terms and transmittal instructions will be appreciated by the occupants of any busy office.

"It is in process" . . . So wrapped up in red tape that the situation is almost hopeless.

"We will look into it" . . . By the time the wheel makes a full turn, we assume you will have forgotten about it, too.

"A program" . . . Any assignment that can't be completed by one telephone call.

"Expedite" . . . To confound confusion with commotion.

"Channels" . . . The trail left by inter-office memos.

"Coordinator" . . . The guy who has a desk between two expeditors.

"Consultant (or expert)" . . . Any ordinary guy with a brief-case, more than 50 miles from home.

"To activate" . . . To make carbons and add more names to the memo.

"To implement a program" . . . Hire more people and expand the office.

"Under consideration" . . . Never heard of it.

"Under active consideration" . . . We're looking in the files for it.

"A meeting" . . . A mass-mulling of master-minds.

"A conference" . . . A place where conversation is substituted for the dreariness of labor and the loneliness of thought.

"To negotiate" . . . To seek a meeting of minds without a knocking together of heads.

"Re-orientation" . . . Getting used to working again.

"Reliable source" . . . The guy you just met.

"Informed source" . . . The guy who told the guy you just met.

"Unimpeachable source" . . . The guy who started the rumor originally.

"A clarification" . . . To fill in the background with so many details that the foreground goes underground.

"We are making a survey" . . . We need more time to think of an answer.

"Note and initial" . . . Let's spread the responsibility for this.

"Let's get together on this" . . . I'm assuming you're as confused as I am.

"See me" or "Let's discuss" . . . Come down to my office, I'm lonesome.

"Give us the benefit of your present thinking" . . . We'll listen to what you have to say, as long as it doesn't interfere with what we have already decided to do.

"We will advise you in due course" . . . If we figure it out, we'll let you know.

"To give someone the picture" . . . A long, confused and inaccurate statement to a newcomer.

"Forwarded for your consideration" . . . You hold the bag for a while.

"Approved, subject to comment" . . . Redraw the D—— thing.

24. Engineers' Dictionary

Each professional discipline has its own special jargon. Engineers and scientists are no exceptions. Within the group, underlying meanings of euphemistic set phrases are perfectly well understood. Such phrases and their meanings are humorously articulated in localized lexicons to be found in laboratories and offices throughout the United States. The following two specimens are representative.

ENGINEERS DICTIONARY

MAJOR TECHNOLOGICAL BREAK-THROUGH.
(Back to the drawing board)

DEVELOPED AFTER YEARS OF INTENSIVE RESEARCH.
(It was discovered by accident)

PROJECT SLIGHTLY BEHIND ORIGINAL SCHEDULE
DUE TO UNFORESEEN DIFFICULTIES.
(We are working on something else)

THE DESIGNS ARE WELL WITHIN ALLOWABLE LIMITS.
(We just made it, stretching a point or two)

CLOSE PROJECT COORDINATION.
(We should have asked someone else . . . . or: Let's spread the
responsibility for this)

CUSTOMER SATISFACTION IS BELIEVED ASSURED.
(We were so far behind schedule that the customer was happy
to get anything at all from us)

THE DESIGN WILL BE FINALIZED IN THE NEXT
REPORTING PERIOD.
(We haven't started this job yet, but we've got to say something)

A NUMBER OF DIFFERENT APPROACHES ARE BEING
TRIED.
(We don't know where we're going, but we're moving)

PRELIMINARY OPERATIONAL TESTS WERE
INCONCLUSIVE.
(The darn thing blew up when we threw the switch)

EXTENSIVE EFFORT IS BEING APPLIED ON A FRESH
APPROACH TO THE PROBLEM.
(We just hired three new guys; we'll let them kick it around for
a while)

TEST RESULTS WERE EXTREMELY GRATIFYING.
(It works and are we surprised!!!)

THE ENTIRE CONCEPT WILL HAVE TO BE ABANDONED.

(The only guy who understood the thing quit)

MODIFICATIONS ARE UNDER WAY TO CORRECT CERTAIN MINOR DIFFICULTIES.

(We threw the whole thing out and are starting from scratch)

A KEY TO SCIENTIFIC RESEARCH LITERATURE[2]

What He Said	What He Meant
It has long been known that . . .	I haven't bothered to look up the original reference but . . .
Of great theoretical and practical importance . . .	Interesting to me.
While it has not been possible to provide definite answers to these questions . . .	The experiment didn't work out, but I figured I could at least get a publication out of it.
The operant conditioning technique was chosen to study the problem . . .	The fellow in the next lab already had the equipment set up.
Three of the Ss were chosen for detailed study . . .	The results on the others didn't make sense.
Typical results are shown . . .	The best results are shown . . .

[2]This item appeared in print in 1962. See Milton H. Hodge, "A Literary Guide for Psychologists," *American Psychologist* 17 (1962): 154. The author mentioned that, in the course of visiting a colleague's laboratory at the University of Georgia, he had been given a glossary of phrases commonly used in scientific reports. He decided to make an abridged version suitable for psychologists, which suggests that Hodge adapted an item already in tradition. Our text is nearly identical to Hodge's, except that Hodge's acknowledgment to Joe Glotz has become one to Joe Clotz, perhaps either because of the typographical similarity between G and C or because of the appropriateness of a name sounding like "klutz," a Yiddish-derived term for a stupid, bumbling person.

Agreement with the predicted curve is:	
excellent	fair
good	poor
satisfactory	doubtful
fair	imaginary
It is suggested that . . . It is believed that . . . It may be that . . .	I think.
It is generally believed that . . .	A couple of other guys think so too.
It is clear that much additional work will be required before a complete understanding . . .	I don't understand it.
Unfortunately, a quantitative theory to account for these results has not been formulated.	I can't think of one and neither has anyone else.
Correct within an order of magnitude . . .	Wrong.
Thanks are due to Joe Clotz for assistance with the experiments and to John Doe for valuable discussion.	Clotz did the work and Doe explained what it meant.

25. Technical Writing Kit

Not only are there ·handy lexicons for jargon, but one finds do-it-yourself aids for the construction of gobbledygook. In the following item found in a computer programmer's office in the Washington, D.C., area in 1972, it becomes astonishingly easy to compose a plausible sounding sample of technical bombast.

TECHNICAL WRITING KIT

This technical writing kit is based on the Simplified Integrated Modular. Prose (SIMP) writing system. Using this kit, anyone who can count to 10 can write up to 40,000 discrete, well-balanced, grammatically correct sentences packed with aerospace terms.

To put SIMP to work, arrange the modules in A-B-C-D order. Take any four-digit number, 8751 for example, and read Phrase 8 off Module A, Phrase 7 off Module B, etc. The result is a SIMP sentence. Add a few more four-digit numbers to make a SIMP paragraph.

After you have mastered the basic technique, you can realize the full potential of SIMP by arranging the modules in D-A-C-B order, B-A-C-D order, or A-B-C-D order. In these advanced configurations, some additional commas may be required.

SIMP Table A

1. In particular,
2. On the other hand,
3. However,
4. Similarly,
5. As a resultant implication,
6. In this regard,
7. Based on integral subsystem considerations,
8. For example,
9. Thus,
0. In respect to specific goals,

SIMP Table B

1. a large portion of the interface coordination communication
2. a constant flow of effective information
3. the characterization of specific criteria
4. initiation of critical subsystem development
5. the fully integrated test program

6. the product configuration baseline
7. any associated supporting element
8. the incorporation of additional mission constraints
9. the independent functional principal
0. a primary interrelationship between system and/or subsystem technologies

---

SIMP Table C

1. must utilize and be functionally interwoven with
2. maximizes the probability of project success and minimizes the cost and time required for
3. adds explicit performance limits to
4. necessitates that urgent consideration be applied to
5. requires considerable systems analysis and trade off studies to arrive at
6. is further compounded, when taking into account
7. presents extremely interesting challenges to
8. recognizes the importance of other systems and the necessity for
9. effects a significant implementation to
0. adds overriding performance constraints to

SIMP Table D

1. the sophisticated hardware
2. the anticipated third generation equipment
3. the subsystem compatibility testing
4. the structural design, based on system engineering concepts
5. the preliminary qualification limit
6. the philosophy of commonality and standardization
7. the evolution of specifications over a given time period
8. the greater flight-worthiness concept
9. any discrete configuration mode
0. the total system rationale

26. Table of Helpful Excuses

One of the hallmarks of American business is efficiency. There is, after all, an entire discipline of "efficiency engineering." One of the common techniques employed by efficiency experts is doing things "by the numbers." In the following exemplar of office folklore, we find typical excuses for *not* being efficient neatly arranged so as to be used more efficiently.

TABLE OF HELPFUL EXCUSES

To save time for management and yourself, please give your excuses by number. The list covers most situations.

1. That's the way we've always done it.
2. I didn't know you were in a hurry for it.
3. That's not my department.
4. No one told me to go ahead.
5. I'm waiting for an O.K.
6. How did I know this was different.
7. That's his job, not mine.
8. Wait 'til the boss comes back and ask him.
9. We don't make many mistakes.
10. I didn't think it was very important.
11. I'm so busy, I just can't get around to it.
12. I thought I told you.
13. I wasn't hired to do that.

27. Political "Isms"

An interesting example of a form perhaps intermediate between definitions and a typology, or, better, a combination definition-typology, is the well-known delineation of political "isms."

The following text dates from the late 1940's and is still current in 1970.

Socialism . . . If you have two cows, you give your neighbor one.

Communism . . . If you have two cows, you give them to the government and the government gives you some milk.

Fascism . . . If you have two cows, you keep the cows and give the milk to the government and the government then sells you some of the milk.

New-Dealism . . . If you have two cows, you shoot one and milk the other and then pour the milk down the drain.

Nazism . . . If you have two cows, the government shoots you and keeps the cows.

Capitalism . . . If you have two cows, you sell one and buy a bull.

28. What the Girls of All Nations Say on the Morning after the Night Before

Equally popular, at least among males, is the set of international ethnic slurs allegedly describing the stereotyped responses of women of different nations after sexual intercourse. Ethnic slurs are often labeled by folklorists with the French technical term *blason populaire*. The people of any given country invariably hold stereotypic notions of the peoples of other countries, not to mention stereotypic notions of subcultures within their own country. One of the principal vehicles for stereotypes is the *blason populaire*. Commonly, they are oral jokes in which representatives from different countries perform a similar activity in accordance with their presumed national characteristics. In this instance, however, the extended list of participants has probably encouraged the written or printed form.

Italian Girl: "Now, you will hate me."

Spanish Girl: "For this I shall love you always."

Russian Girl: "My body has belonged to you, but my soul shall always remain free."

German Girl: "After we rest awhile, maybe we go to a Beer Garden, Yah!"

Swedish Girl: "I tank I go home now."

French Girl: "For this I get new dress, Wee?"

Colored Girl: "Boss, ah sho hope this done change yo luck."

Chinese Girl: "Now you know it isn't so."

English Girl: "Rather pleasant, don't you know; we try again. Tallyho."

American Girl: "I'll be damned. I must have been drunk. What did you say your name was?"

The stereotypes are quite conventional. There is the beer-drinking German, the French interest in elegant dress, the English penchant for understatement and love of sport, and so on. The American stereotype suggests the casualness of sexual relationships and the necessity of liquor for weakening inhibitions. The implication that the American girl has no recollection of the act is an extreme example of the notion that American women do not enjoy sex or participate voluntarily in sexual activities.

29. Types of Men One Meets in a Washroom

A classic example of a traditional typology that also reflects the American obsession with bodily functions and bathroom behavior provides personality thumbnail sketches of male urinators. Since American children are taught from infancy on that body products are "dirty" and that the actions connected with defecation and urination are likewise dirty, it is difficult for many adults to feel comfortable when using a public restroom. (The very use of such euphemisms as rest room, washroom, powder room, etc., indicates a lack of frankness. After all, one does not rest in a rest room or take a bath in a public *bath*room. Note that the term "lavatory" literally refers to washing, but one rarely goes into a washroom just to wash!) Moreover, just as most men hope no one is watching them urinate and pretend not to be observing their neighbor standing at the adjacent urinal, the fact is that one observes and is observed.[3] This ordinarily taboo subject is considered in detail in the following typology:

TYPES OF MEN ONE MEETS IN A WASHROOM

1. *Excitable*: Shorts half twisted around, cannot find hole, rips shorts.
2. *Sociable*: Joins friends in a piss whether he has to go or not.
3. *Cross-eyed*: Looks into urinal on the left, pisses into one in center, flushes one on right.
4. *Nosey*: Looks into next urinal to see how other guy is fixed.
5. *Timid*: Cannot urinate if someone is watching, flushes urinal as if he has already used it, sneaks back later.
6. *Indifferent*: All urinals being used, pisses in sink.
7. *Clever*: No hands, shows off by fixing tie, looks around, pisses on shoe.
8. *Worried*: Is not sure of what he has been into lately, makes quick inspection.
9. *Frivolous*: Plays stream up and down and across urinal, tries to hit fly, never grows up.
10. *Absent-minded*: Opens vest, pulls out tie, pisses in pants.
11. *Disgruntled*: Stands for a while, gives up, walks away.
12. *Sneak*: Farts silently while leaking, acts very innocent, knows man in next stall will be blamed.
13. *Childish*: Looks directly into bottom of urinal, likes to see it bubble.
14. *Patient*: Stands very close for a long time waiting, reads newspaper with free hand.
15. *Desperate*: Waits in long line, teeth floating, pisses in pants.

[3] For a further consideration of American public bathroom behavior, see Alan Dundes, "Here I Sit—A Study of American Latrinalia," *Papers of the Kroeber Anthropological Society* 34 (1966): 91–105.

16. *Efficient*: Waits until he has to crap, then does both jobs.
17. *Tough*: Bangs dick against side of urinal to dry it.
18. *Fat*: Has to back up and take long blind shot at urinal, misses, pisses on shoe.
19. *Little*: Stands on box, falls in, drowns.
20. *Drunk*: Holds left thumb in right hand, pisses in pants.

Much of the behavior appears to be quite regressive inasmuch as it depends upon a "loss-of-control" theme reminiscent of infancy when children invariably have accidents along the path to proper bathroom behavior. Occasionally versions of this typology are accompanied by cartoon drawings.

CONCEITED MAN: Acts as though he is in deep thought. Stands up to urinal and stretches it out as far as he can, glances over to the fellow next to him to see if he is looking. Wants him to think he has something. Ordinarily looks like two belly buttons. Puts it away quickly. Whistles nervously.

INDIFFERENT MAN: All urinals busy, pisses in sink.

ABSENT-MINDED MAN: Rus es in, opens vest, takes o tie, looks in mirror, pisses pants.

FAT MAN: Always wondering where stream is going. Pisses on floor, stray stream usually hits outside of pants. Never knows about shoes until he gets outside. Kicks left leg out to bat balls in place. Walks out smiling with fly open.

FRIVOLOUS MAN: Plays the stream up and down and across the urinal trying to write his initials. Attempts to hit flies. This type never grows up.

CLEVER MAN: No ha showing off, hands in pockets, looks at ceiling, ually pisses on shoes.

CROSS-EYED MAN: Looks into urinal at left, leaks into one in center, flushes one at right.

PERSONALITY MAN: Tells dirty jokes while pissing. Has pronounced control over farts. Farts at will. Has fellows in stitches.

ORRIED MAN: Isn't sure at he has been into lately, kes frenzied search and inection. Usually whistles.

SNEAKY MAN: Farts silently while leaking, looks innocent, figures it will be blamed on fellow next to him.

CHILDISH MAN: Leaks directly into the bottom of bowl. Likes to hear splatter.

30. Types of Girls in the Powder Room

Since American girls are exposed to the same strict toilet training as American boys, they too grow up to be uncomfortable in public rest rooms. It is not clear, however, whether the following typology was composed originally by a male or a female. It is possible that it is more commonly circulated among males than females. In any case, in both the male and female typologies is an air of bravado about an act that is normally carried out privately and quietly. It should also be pointed out that individual toilet behavior probably *is* indicative of actual adult personality configurations, though not necessarily those presented in the following caricature.

Cautious Girl: Has heard of some girls contracting V.D. from toilet seats, she straddles bowl, leans over to flush toilet and pees on new nylons.

Indifferent Girl: Rushes in, lifts dress, pulls pantie crotch aside and just lets go. Sounds like a bucket of water being poured out of a third-story window.

Worried Girl: A week "past-due," visits powder room every hour, sits down, uses toilet paper and looks for encouraging design, walks out biting nails.

President's Secretary: Has key to the "can," walks in, gives other girls the "'high-hat"; this type farts louder than a fire cracker and stinks worse than a goat.

Sloppy Girl: Pees all over front of the toilet seat. Is halfway out of the powder room before she notices panties down around her ankles.

Sophisticated Girl: Seldom wears pants, never knows when she will meet a man.

Bashful Girl: Looks under "privy door" to see if anyone else is in the powder room. If not alone, sits down, holds handle on toilet seat flush for constant flow of water; pees quietly, coughs, hums and ends up with a loud fart after the water has stopped flushing. She walks out blushing.

Acrobatic Girl: Stands up with one foot on toilet seat and in this position emits a straight-forward stream. This type is about as tight as the inside of a size 8 derby hat.

Cross-eyed Girl: Sits with one cheek on side of seat and in this position pees all over the floor, usually wears galoshes on her visit to the can.

Frivolous Girl: Lets stream go in little squirts to the tune of "Little-toot," whistles while she wee wees.

Literary Girl: Always takes "Book of the Month" to powder room; sits in can and reads; blames the book *Forever Amber* for her piles.

Big Timer: Always leaves toilet door open while she chats and brags to other girls about the guy she took on the night before. Shows girls panties with black lace edging and "WEL-COME" embroidered in crotch. Has never been in bed with a man.

Absent-Minded Girl: Forgets she has snuggies on; pees on herself before she can get the damn things off.

As in the case of the male washroom typology, versions of the female powder-room typology have circulated accompanied by cartoon illustrations.

CAUTIOUS GIRL
Has heard of so many girls contracting V.D. from toilet seats, lifts seat, straddles bowl, leans over to flush toilet and pees all over her brand new nylons.

INDIFFERENT GIRL
Rushes in, lifts dress, pulls panties crotch aside and just lets go. Sounds like a bucket of water being poured out a third story window.

WORRIED GIRL
A week "past due," visits powder room every hour, sits down, uses toilet paper, looks for encouraging red designs and walks out biting nails.

PRESIDENT'S SECRETAR
Hastens to own private "ca Walks in giving other g "highhat." This type l louder than a firecracker stinks worse than a goat.

FRIVOLOUS GIRL
Lets stream go in squirts to tune of "Little Toot Toot." Whistles while she wee's.

CROSS-EYED GIRL
Sits with half-an-ass on side of seat and pees all over the floor. Usually wears galoshes on visits to the "can."

BASHFUL GIRL
Looks under "private doors" to see if anyone else is in the powder room—if not alone, sits down, holds handle on toilet seat, flushes for constant flow of water, pees quietly, coughs, hums, and ends up with a loud fart after water has ceased flushing, she walks out blushing.

ACROBATIC GIRL
Stands up with one foot toilet seat, and, in this pe tion, emits a straight do ward stream. This type about as tight as the inside a size 8 derby hat.

BIG TIME
Always leaves toilet door open while she chats and brags about the guy she took home the night before. Shows girls panties with black lace edging and "Welcome" embroidered on crotch. Has never slept with a man.

ABSENT-MINDED GIRL
Forgets she has on snuggies, pees all over herself before she gets the damn things off.

TEEN-AGE GIRL
Likes to see her own smile of relief, also to imitate big brother, generally ignores the comfort of toilet seat, and does it the hard way by straddling wash sink.

HILLBILLY GIRL
Never uses modern toilet says she can't get the pro musical tones she plays wi taking a good pee. Carries own basket with her where she pees.

31. Murphy's Laws

In all the folk attempts to arrive at definitions and typologies one finds a hint of the influence of modern science. Scientific descriptions and classifications are to be found in nearly every scientific discipline. One of the most fascinating of all the examples of urban folklore consists of a parody of scientific laws. Often termed "Murphy's Laws," it is also known under the title of "Finagle's Laws," with "Finagle" being an obvious play on the word "finagle," meaning to achieve something by deception or fraud. Analogous slang terms include the "fudge" factor and the "diddle" factor.

Murphy's Laws draw a bead on the American mania for scientific certainty. In reading Murphy's Laws, it is well to remember that a definite ideological commitment to such values as optimism, progress, and efficiency in addition to the principles of pure science exists in American ideal culture. Clearly, Murphy's Laws constitute a folk corrective to norms of ideal culture, coming reasonably close, we feel, to real, rather than ideal, culture. Americans may fear failure, but, if they can *successfully* codify the principles underlying failure, failure becomes predictable and what is predictable is further proof of the validity of an objective, scientific worldview.

Murphy's Laws are also concerned with the American's love of success and his wish that experiments come out right. Interestingly enough, the implications of Murphy's Laws for American worldview have been discussed by scientists themselves. Scientists, it turns out, are perhaps the most ardent admirers of Murphy's Laws. For example, in one of many discussions occurring in the letters-to-the-editor column in a popular science-fiction magazine, the differences between the Finagle factor, the Bugger (or Fudge) factor, and the Diddle factor are delineated. Taking a mathematical equation as a point of departure, it is argued that the Finagle factor is characterized by changing the

universe to fit the equation. The Bugger or Fudge factor changes
the equation to fit the universe. And the Diddle factor changes
things so that the equation and the universe appear to fit, without making any real change in either.[^4] Obviously all these alternatives are making fun of American scientists' propensity for con-
structing equations or models that are supposed to represent the
nature of reality. American empiricism demands that the models
or hypotheses be tested. To the extent that the model matches
(or explains) natural phenomena, it is a successful model. The
situation is a bit like what occurs when theory and data don't
confirm one another. One can keep the theory and reject the
data; one can reject or modify the theory and keep the data; or
one can juggle the theory and juggle the data to make it look as
though they fit one another. Finally, Murphy's Laws demonstrate
the American delight in parody. It is the possibility of self-analy-
sis through parody that keeps Americans from taking themselves
too seriously.

The following text contains only one of Murphy's Laws, the
most common one, plus a group of analogous laws and axioms.

BASIC PRECEPTS OF SCIENCE

MURPHY'S LAW: If anything can go wrong, it will.

PATRICK'S THEOREM: If the experiment works, you must be using
    the wrong equipment.

SKINNER'S CONSTANT: That quantity which, when multiplied
    times, divided into, added to, or subtracted from the answer
    you got, gives the answer you should have gotten.

HORNER'S FIVE THUMB POSTULATE: Experience varies directly
    with equipment ruined.

FLAGLE'S LAW OF THE PERVERSITY OF INANIMATE OBJECTS: Any
    inanimate object, regardless of its composition or configura-
    tion, may be expected to perform at any time in a totally un-

[^4]: See *Astounding Science Fiction* 60 (1958): 155.

expected manner for reasons that are either totally obscure or completely mysterious.

ALLEN's AXIOM: When all else fails, read the instructions.

THE SPARE PARTS PRINCIPLE: The accessibility, during recovery, of small parts which fall from the work bench, varies directly with the size of the part . . . and inversely with its importance to the completion of the work underway.

THE COMPENSATION COROLLARY: The experiment may be considered a success if no more than 50% of the observed measurements must be discarded to obtain a correspondence with theory.

GUMPERSON's LAW: The probability of a given event occurring is inversely proportional to its desirability.

THE ORDERING PRINCIPLE: Those supplies necessary for yesterday's experiment must be ordered no later than tomorrow noon.

THE ULTIMATE PRINCIPLE: By definition, when you are investigating the unknown, you do not know what you will find.

THE FUTILITY FACTOR: No experiment is ever a complete failure . . . it can always serve as a bad example.

Another version of the list of scientific precepts is specifically entitled Murphy's Laws. It was copied off the bulletin board at the Protein Chemistry Lab at the Massachusetts General Hospital in Boston in the spring of 1968.

MURPHY'S LAWS

1. In any field of scientific endeavor, anything that can go wrong, will go wrong;
2. Left to themselves, things always go from bad to worse;
3. If there is a possibility of several things going wrong, the one that will go wrong is the one that will do the most damage;
4. Nature always sides with the hidden flaw;
5. Mother Nature is a Bitch;
6. If everything seems to be going well, you have obviously overlooked something.

Still another version of Murphy's Laws indicates the great variety of principles. Nevertheless, all the versions seem to have the same initial law. This version was collected from the wall of the anthropology departmental office at the University of Utah in April, 1969.

MURPHY'S LAWS

A set of maxims that seems to fill the gaps between all the laws, rules, and regulations governing and explaining human behavior:

If anything can go wrong, it will.

Nothing is as simple as it seems.

Everything always costs more money than you have.

Everything takes longer than you expect.

If you fool around with something long enough, it will eventually break.

If you try to please everybody, somebody is not going to like it.

It is a fundamental law of nature that nothing ever quite works out.

Whatever you want to do, you have to do something else first.

It's easier to get into a thing than to get out of it.

If you explain something so clearly that no one can misunderstand, someone will.

❁   ❁   ❁   ❁   ❁

To which we can add only that if anyone thinks Mr. Murphy was kidding, he must not have been around very long.

32. Murphy's Laws for Construction Engineers

A localization of Murphy's Laws found in Lafayette, California, is evidently directed toward construction engineering and contracting. Accompanying the laws is a business-card-sized certificate form that reads as follows:

International Society of
PHILOSOPHICAL ENGINEERS
3.1416 Hogwash Ave., Lafayette, Calif.

This is to Certify that
_____ No._____
Having successfully passed a thorough examination
on Finagle's Law, misreading blueprints and
underestimating costs and competition, is
hereby entitled to practice all forms of
shade tree engineering, advanced sidewalk
superintending and do-it-yourself construction.

Bougar T. Factor, Pres.   Flywheel Bushing, Sec.

Note that the address includes the numerical figure 3.1416 for
the constant pi and that the name of the chairman or president
is Bougar T. Factor, a thinly disguised rewriting of the "Bugger
Factor."

THE RECOMMENDED PRACTICES COMMITTEE
of the
INTERNATIONAL SOCIETY OF PHILOSOPHICAL ENGINEERS
presents
A Compilation of Finagle's Universal Laws for Naive Engineers

Axiom # 1:   In any calculation, any error which can creep in
will do so.

Axiom # 2:   Any error in any calculation will be in the direction of most harm.

Axiom # 3:   In any formula, constants (especially those obtained from engineering hand-books) are to be
treated as variables.

Axiom # 4:   The best approximation of service conditions in
the laboratory will not begin to meet those conditions encountered in actual service.

Axiom # 5:   The most vital dimension on any plan or drawing stands the greatest chance of being omitted.

Axiom # 6:   If only one bid can be secured on any project, the price will be unreasonable.

Axiom # 7:   If a test installation functions perfectly, all subsequent production units will malfunction.

Axiom # 8:   All delivery promises must be multiplied by a factor of 2.0.

Axiom # 9:   Major changes in construction will always be requested after fabrication is nearly completed.

Axiom # 10:   Parts that positively cannot be assembled in improper order will be.

Axiom # 11:   Interchangeable parts won't.

Axiom # 12:   Manufacturer's specifications of performance should be multiplied by a factor of 0.5.

Axiom # 13:   Salesmen's claims for performance should be multiplied by a factor of 0.25.

Axiom # 14:   Installation and Operating Instructions shipped with any device will be promptly discarded by the Receiving Department.

Axiom # 15:   Any device requiring service or adjustment will be least accessible.

Axiom # 16:   Service Conditions as given on specifications will be exceeded.

Axiom # 17:   If more than one person is responsible for a miscalculation, no one will be at fault.

Axiom # 18:   Identical units which test in an identical fashion will not behave in an identical fashion in the field.

Axiom # 19:   If, in engineering practice, a safety factor is set through service experience at an ultimate value, an ingenious idiot will promptly calculate a method to exceed said safety factor.

Axiom # 20:   Warranty and guarantee clauses are voided by payment of the invoice.

Note: While the accuracy of the above Axioms is vouched for, the Committee does not feel that this compilation is by any means complete. The

Committee will welcome any additions conforming to good philosophical engineering practice to the list.

Bougar T. Factor, Chairman

Novel Notices and
Memorable Memos

It should be clear by now that nearly all the material presented thus far is transmitted by office workers. Admittedly, most of the items are probably run off or copied sub rosa since in theory the xerox machine is supposed to be reserved for official office business. Since an increasing number of Americans either work in or have contact with some kind of office, the office as an institution has become more and more important, and it is not surprising that office life itself is described in written urban folklore. Specifically, the employer-employee relationship serves as the focus of a large variety of texts. With the plethora of official memoranda and instructions governing all phases of employee activity, it is entirely appropriate that employees fight fire with fire by responding in kind.

33. I'm Not Allowed to Run the Train

One of the most common complaints among employees of any company concerns the lack of freedom to make decisions or to exercise initiative, particularly at the lower levels of the organizational hierarchy. Conformity rather than innovation is encouraged by a host of "standard operating procedures," instructions, and guidelines designed to limit the margin of employee error and to produce maximum efficiency. On the other hand, when things go wrong, there is often an attempt to select a scapegoat from the lower portions of the echelon. In effect, an employee may be punished for simply carrying out orders given by his supervisor.

A short but eloquent poetic protest against the restrictions and unreason of "the system" has been found in such widely diverse environments as the bulletin board of a restaurant in the resort community of Mono Hot Springs, California, and in an intelligence computer room at the Naval Station at Sanford, Florida.

> I AM NOT ALLOWED TO RUN THE TRAIN
> THE WHISTLE I CANNOT BLOW
> I'M NOT THE ONE WHO DESIGNATES
> HOW FAR THE TRAIN WILL GO
> I'M NOT ALLOWED TO LET OFF STEAM
> OR EVEN RING THE BELL
> BUT LET THE TRAIN JUST JUMP THE TRACK
> AND SEE WHO CATCHES HELL.

34. Positions to Be Eliminated

The fear of sudden unemployment is a constant one in an age of increasing automation and fluctuating levels of personnel needs. Employees in industries dependent upon government contracts are particularly vulnerable to shifts in legislative appropriations.

The following text expresses this fear and at the same time pokes fun at the American penchant for acronymic abbreviations.[1] Once again we find the common practice of describing employee anxieties in sexual terms.

Notice

MANY POSITIONS TO BE ELIMINATED BY MID-1967

In view of the 10% reduction of the budget, the California State Civil Service Commission will apply its RAPE program to all branches of the State Government by midsummer of 1967, according to Governor Reagan. Particular emphasis of the program will be placed on the Transportation Branch. RAPE is the designation for the phase-out of many departments and stands for "Retire All Personnel Early."

Employees who are RAPED will have an opportunity to seek other employment. Those who decline to seek other employment will be able to request a review of their records before discharge. This phase of the cut-back is dubbed SCREW (Survey of Capabilities of Retired Early Workers).

One additional opportunity is promised by the Government for employees who have been RAPED or SCREWED. They may appeal for a final review . . . SHAFT. (Study by Higher Authority Following Termination.)

Governor Reagan explained that employees who are RAPED are allowed only one additional SCREWING but may request the SHAFT as many times as they desire.

[1] There are a number of variants of this item, one dating from 1965. A version dated 1970 is addressed to "All Elderly Employees" where a task force known as the CRAP group (Commission to Review Activities in Personnel) phases out older employees. The RAPE program in this version refers to "Retired Aged Personnel Early." Another version allegedly from the Naval Weapons Center in Washington, D.C. (in 1968), labels its RAPE phase-out as "Reassignment, Attrition, and Personnel Elimination." SCREW is "survey of capabilities for reassignment of eliminated workers." The final paragraph reads: "Personnel not affected by this order, those who have been neither RAPED nor SCREWED, shall henceforth be designated Veteran Incumbents Retained in the Good Interests of the NAVAL Service (VIRGINS)."

35. Guide to Employee Performance Appraisal

Another area of employee concern is the evaluation procedure. Advancement, promotion, and pay raises frequently depend upon a favorable recommendation by one's superior. The criteria for employee performance are not always very explicit. However, some companies have instituted employee-evaluation check sheets somewhat analogous to fitness-report forms for officers in the military. The following evaluation parody takes as its point of departure the comic-strip character of Superman who was always introduced as being "faster than a speeding bullet, more powerful than a locomotive, able to leap tall buildings at a single bound." This parody shows the impact of mass popular culture upon the content of folklore (although, to be sure, the character and plot of Superman comics are themselves derived in part from folkloristic hero cycles).

One feature of the appraisal guide is the necessity for superlatives in personnel evaluations. If a worker (or colleague) is labeled "competent" (e.g., "meets job requirements"), this means that he is being judged as mediocre. To call someone competent is thus to damn with faint praise. The American insistence upon exaggeration, be it in the tall tale or in the "best hot dog in the world" type of advertising, is definitely a factor in employee evaluation. The fact that there are five degrees of performance reminds us of the five-grade system in education: A, B, C, D, and F.

GUIDE TO EMPLOYEE PERFORMANCE APPRAISAL

PERFORMANCE DEGREES

Performance Factors	Far Exceeds Job Requirements	Exceeds Job Requirements	Meets Job Requirements	Needs Some Improvement	Does Not Meet Minimum Requirements
Quality	Leaps tall buildings with a single bound.	Must take running start to leap over tall buildings.	Can only leap over a short building or medium with no spires.	Crashes into buildings when attempting to jump over them.	Cannot recognize buildings at all, much less jump.
Timeliness	Is faster than a speeding bullet.	Is as fast as a speeding bullet.	Not quite as fast as a speeding bullet.	Would you believe a slow bullet?	Wounds self with bullet when attempting to shoot gun.
Initiative	Is stronger than a locomotive.	Is stronger than a bull elephant.	Is stronger than a bull.	Shoots the bull.	Smells like a bull.
Adaptability	Walks on water consistently.	Walks on water in emergencies.	Washes with water.	Drinks water.	Passes water in emergencies.
Communication	Talks with God.	Talks with the Angels.	Talks to himself.	Argues with himself.	Loses these arguments.

36. A Parable of Personnel Policy

The previous text made specific allusion to talking to God and walking on water. The relationship between Christianity and capitalism is once again made explicit. Another means of comparing American religion and American business is the casting of a business parody in the form of a psalm or a religious parable. In this way, misusing sick leave and arriving on the job drunk are depicted as modern-day sins.

> And it came to pass that the Director of Personnel appeared before them and showed unto them the office and the wonders thereof: and caused them to know the size of their pay-checks, and that after they had labored for the project for six months they would accumulate 5 days of vacation time and of sick leave 48 hours; and that this should continue as long as the sun should rise and set and they should continue upon the Staff. But the director saw in his heart that they panted not after self-improvement nor sought to learn each of them how he could best help the Audit Staff, but rather lusted after their pay-checks, and their vacation time, and their sick leave—how they would spend them. And he was wroth and he prophesied unto them, saying: Take ye not your vacation time without the permission of your master, lest he be offended at thee and call thee unto his office and mash thy tail heavily. Better that thou shouldst be gone three weeks, even a month or more at a time, than that thou shouldst fail to show up on a day when thy presence is expected and dirty work a-waiteth upon thy desk to be done in haste.
>
> Woe be unto him who taketh of his sick leave as it accrues, for it shall be remembered against him. Yea, even tho he be suffering unto the point of death, it shall be remembered against him, and his days shall be numbered, and his path shall lead but unto the way of misfortune and unto the shadow of the list. Verily, I say unto thee, that once thy

name is entered on the list that thy name may pass in time
to the head of the roster and become as a title thereon for
all to read as they sit in conclave at the time of the passing
out of the pay raises. And I say unto thee that it shall come
to pass that if one of you shall in anywise remain at his
home, or at a hospital, or at the office of a physician or an
undertaker, and shall call in unto thy master's office saying
in a weak voice, "Master, I am ill and suffer greatly, and
shall appear not at the place of my laboring until after the
rising of tomorrow's sun." Then shalt thou be subjected to
great suspicion. Upon thy return thy breath shall be smelled
of, and thy tongue, the furriness thereof, be inspected, and
thou shalt be entered at once and in great haste upon the
list, and thy master shall speak to thee not . . . when thou
cometh upon him in the washroom, and from that day hence
thy name shall be as mud.

And he spake unto them again, saying: Take not thy sick
leave upon the opening day of fishing season, or the season
for the hunting of the stag, or of the duck, nor even the
quail or the dove, lest thou come suddenly upon thy master
using up his sick leave, and seeing him not in time, he shall
retire to a place of privacy behind a bush or a rock and shall
write thy name upon his list, and thou shalt live to regret
the day. For from that day forward thy time shalt be a time
of suffering and great unrest, and thy soul shall sit in fear
and trembling within the cage of thy ribs, and thy hindquarters shall become wary and hard to approach, but thy boss
shall ride thereon daily. And thou shalt cry unto thy wife at
eventide, saying: "Mary, the hand of the boss is heavy upon
me and his heart is turned against me for I am upon his list
and he forgetteth not the day of my sick leave, and when
cometh the time of the year when the merit increases are
passed among my brethren, yea, then he holdeth back the
sheckels in his hand until I have passed by in the line and
he giveth them unto the hand of one of the Brown Nose
tribe: verily, I work like a dog for peanuts," thou shalt say,
and more too, and thy wife shall feel exceeding grief for
the lacerations of thy soul, and shall weep with thee, and

shall say unto thee: "Oh, John, let us flee this awful place and return again home."

And it shall come to pass in those days that thou shalt write an epistle of farewell to thy master, saying, "Boss, fourteen times shall the sun rise upon this Laboratory, and fourteen times shall it set, and I shall still be with thee, but upon the fifteenth rising of the sun, I shall go forth from under thine hand and shall shake the dust of this place from out of my sandals and return unto the land from whence I came, and shall return not." And further thou shalt say: "Boss, since I took that day's sick leave, thy face has been turned from me, and thy hand has been set against me, and thy foot has been upon my neck. Even as a love-child at a family reunion is treated, so have I been treated, until my soul is sore. I have feared to rest from my labors for even the span of a gnat's sneeze, lest thou come upon me unawares from behind and gnaw upon my hindquarters to the delight of all within earshot. Yea, even tho I may pass through the valley of the shadow of death, I would fear to pause to tremble, for I know that thou followest hard upon my heels, and I fear no evil like the glint in thine eye. And shouldst thou lead me into green pastures and beside the still waters, I would dare not lay me down to rest therein, lest thou pounce upon me and mash my tail in the presence of mine enemies, and cause me to utter loud lamentations for all to marvel at." And so saying, thou shalt resign.

And the Director of Personnel, seeing that they were much impressed and depressed, folded his arms across his chest, and spoke even more sternly unto them, saying:

And if in these times it shall come to pass that thy master shall come not into his place of the flinging of the authority, yea, even unto his office of administration and supervision, if he shall come not for a day, or two days, or three, or even unto the span of a week, but shall lie heavily in his bed and tell his wife to call into the master of the masters and report of his sickness, then shalt thou go quietly and respectfully about the doing of thy labors and mutter not about thy master, lest thy mutterings fall upon the ears of an eager Stool

Pigeon and be repeated by him in high places to thy great
undoing, and shouldst thou feel the word "Hangover" rising
to the tip of thy tongue, reach thou in quickly and yank out
thy tongue by its roots, lest it get thee into a mess like unto
that in Hades.

And so saying, he departed from among them and took
himself unto the cafeteria for a cup of coffee. And they
marvelled greatly among themselves at the manner and in-
tent of his speaking.

END OF PARABLE

37. Those Good Old Days

The promulgation of guidelines for employee behavior is nothing new. The following example purports to be a statement of
desired employee conduct in effect around the time of the Civil
War. Different versions refer to 1872 and 1862, though, of course,
they may have been composed much later. The nostalgia implicit
in the phrase "good old days" is belied by the strictness of the
rules set forth.

The Boston Globe recently printed a copy of a set of office
rules posted in 1872 by the owner of a carriage works to guide
his white collar workers. We think you will find them of interest.

1. Office employees will daily sweep the floors, dust the furniture, shelves, and showcases.
2. Each day fill lamps, clean chimneys, and trim wicks. Wash
the windows once a week.
3. Each clerk will bring in a bucket of water and scuttle of
coal for the day's business.
4. Make your pens carefully. You may whittle nibs to your individual taste.
5. This office will open at 7:00 A.M. and close at 8:00 P.M. ex-

cept on the Sabbath, on which day we will remain closed. Each employee is expected to spend the Sabbath by attending church and contributing liberally to the cause of the Lord.

6. Men employees will be given an evening off each week for courting purposes, or two evenings a week if they go regularly to church.

7. After an employee has spent his 13 hours of labor in the office, he should spend the remaining time reading the Bible and other good books.

8. Every employee should lay aside from each pay a goodly sum of his earnings for his benefit during his declining years, so that he will not become a burden on society or his betters.

9. Any employee who smokes Spanish cigars, uses liquor in any form, or frequents pool and public halls, or gets shaved in a barber shop, will give me good reason to suspect his worth, intentions, integrity, and honesty.

10. The employee who has performed his labors faithfully without a fault for five years will be given an increase of five cents per day in his pay, providing profits from the business permit it.

38. Instructions on Death of Employees

It is not only performance that is noticed by office supervisors, but also nonperformance. Some employees elect to do the minimum or may be unable to be very productive, the "dead wood" of any large organization. The following "Instructions on Death of Employees" shows folk recognition of minimal performance and the philosophy of doing "just enough to get by."

August 28, 1968
Re: Death of Employees

To: All Personnel
From: Your Big Brother

Instructions on Death of Employees:

It has been brought to the attention of this office that many employees have been dying while on duty for apparently no good reason. Further, some employees are refusing to fall over after they are dead. This, in some cases, has resulted in unearned overtime payments which do not fit into our company program.

Effective immediately—this practice must be discontinued.

On and after today, any employee found sitting up after he has died will be dropped from the payroll at once, without investigation under Regulation No. 20, Section D (non-productive labor).

The following procedure will be strictly adhered to:

If, after several hours, it is noted that any employee has not moved or opened at least one eye, the Department Head will investigate. Because of the highly sensitive nature and origin of some employees and the close resemblance between death and their normal working attitude, the investigation will be made quietly to avoid waking the employee if he or she is asleep (which is permitted under the present regime and union contract). If some doubt exists as to the true condition of the employee, a pay check will be used as the final test. If the employee fails to reach for the check, it is reasonable to assume that death has occurred.

NOTE: In some cases, the instinct is so strongly developed that a spasmodic clutching action may occur. Do not be misled by this manifestation.

In the event that any employee fails to abandon whatever he is doing when it comes time for coffee break, no investigation is necessary, as this is conclusive proof that rigor mortis has set in.

39. New Sick-Leave Policy

If some employees do too little, it is also true that some employers demand too much. A *reductio ad absurdum* of the overstrict employer is illustrated in the following memorandum.

TO ALL PERSONNEL

Subject: New Sick Leave Policy

It has been brought to my attention that the attendance record of the department is a disgrace. It has become necessary for us to revise some of our policies. The following changes are in effect as of today:

SICKNESS: No excuse . . . We will no longer accept your doctor's statement as proof, as we feel that if you are able to go to the doctor, you are able to come to work.

DEATHS: (Other than your own) . . . This is no excuse. There is nothing you can do for them, and we are sure that someone with a lesser position can attend to the arrangements. However, if the funeral can be held in the late afternoon, we will be glad to let you off one hour early provided that your job is far enough ahead to keep going in your absence.

LEAVES OF ABSENCE: (For an operation) . . . We are no longer allowing this practice, as we wish to discourage any thoughts that you may have to have an operation as we believe that as long as you are an employee here that you will need all of whatever you have and you should not consider having anything removed. We hired you as you are and to have anything removed would certainly make you less than we bargained for.

DEATH: (Your own) . . . This will be accepted as an excuse, but we would like a two-weeks notice as we feel it is your duty to train someone else for your job.

NOTE: There is also entirely too much time being spent in the restrooms. In the future, we will follow the practice of going in alphabetical order. For instance, those whose names begin with "A" will go from 8:00 to 8:15 A.M., "B" will go from 8:15 to 8:30 A.M., and so on. If you are unable to go at your specified time, it will be necessary to wait until the next day when your turn comes around again.

The Management

40. The Order

If some employees are insufficiently motivated in the performance of their assigned duties, others are over-zealous, particularly in sales activities where participants work on a commission basis. The following example is once again in pseudo-parable form. Notice the indictment of the practice of making excessively low bids to secure contracts. Such a practice, like a sudden "gas war" (which occurs when two or more gas stations start cutting their price rates for gasoline in an effort to corner all the business), may reduce or all but eliminate any chance for a profit. And, in the United States, a profit is not without honor. In fact, it is the lack of profit that is a disgrace in terms of American business philosophy.

The Order

How IT CAME TO PASS, a great prophet once addressed a herd of donkeys.

"What would a donkey require for a three-day journey?" And they answered, "Six bundles of hay and three bags of dates."

"That soundeth like a fair price, but I have for only one of you a three-day journey and I cannot give six bundles of hay and three bags of dates. Who will go for less?"

Behold ALL STOOD FORTH.

One would go for six bundles of hay and two bags of dates, another for three bundles and one bag. Now one especially long-eared donkey agreed to go for one bundle of hay.

Whereupon THE PROPHET REPLIED:

"Thou art a disgrace to the herd and an Ass. Thou cannot live for three days on one bundle of hay, much less undertake the journey and profit thereby."

"True," replied the Ass, hanging his long ears in shame.

"But I wanted to get the order."

AUTHOR UNKNOWN

41. The Rush-Job Calendar

Americans are prisoners of time. They live in a world of deadlines and due dates. Actually, most of the peoples of the world tend to be past-oriented rather than future-oriented. In a past-oriented society, the old way is best, and more effort is spent in observing tradition than in departing from it. Americans, in contrast, prefer the new rather than the old and look forward to a bigger and better future.[2] If Americans look back at tradition, it is probably with the idea of replacing or updating it.

In the following piece of calendrical fantasy, a number of important themes of American culture are evident. Americans do have a fast pace of life in comparison with other peoples. Americans race and rush in almost all their activities. Saving time is a common goal, and most industries pride themselves on time-saving devices or routines. Efficiency and productivity, two other highly valued characteristics, are measured in part along a time axis. Thus, through technology, Americans attempt to manipulate time for their own profit. This tendency is carried to a point of *reductio ad absurdum* in this imaginary calendar. Noteworthy is the fact that the instructions accompanying the calendar indicate some of the critical days in American life; for instance, the tenth day of the month is customarily the last date of the grace period for payments due on the first of the month, with a penalty incurred if payment is made after the tenth.

[2]For a further consideration of this tendency, see Alan Dundes, "Thinking Ahead: A Folkloristic Reflection of the Future Orientation in American Worldview," *Anthropological Quarterly* 42 (1969): 53–72.

RUSH JOB CALENDAR

NEG	FRI	FRI	THU	WED	TUE	MON
8	7	6	5	4	3	2
16	15	14	13	12	11	9
23	22	21	20	19	18	17
31	30	29	28	27	26	24
38	37	36	35	34	33	32

1. EVERY JOB IS IN A RUSH. EVERYONE WANTS HIS JOB YESTERDAY. WITH THIS CALENDAR, A CUSTOMER CAN ORDER HIS WORK ON THE 7TH AND HAVE IT DELIVERED ON THE 3RD.

2. ALL CUSTOMERS WANT THEIR JOBS ON FRIDAY SO THERE ARE TWO FRIDAYS IN EVERY WEEK.

3. THERE ARE SEVEN DAYS AT THE END OF THE MONTH FOR THOSE END-OF-MONTH JOBS.

4. THERE WILL BE NO FIRST-OF-THE-MONTH BILLS TO BE PAID AS THERE ISN'T ANY "FIRST". THE "TENTH" AND "TWENTY-FIFTH" ALSO HAVE BEEN OMITTED IN CASE YOU HAVE BEEN ASKED TO PAY THEM ONE OF THOSE DAYS.

5. THERE ARE NO BOTHERSOME NON-PRODUCTIVE SATURDAYS AND SUNDAYS. NO TIME-AND-A-HALF OR DOUBLE TIME TO PAY.

6. THERE'S A NEW DAY EACH WEEK CALLED NEGOTIATION DAY.

A very different version of the warped calendar has been localized for forest rangers.

WORK IMPROVEMENT SUGGESTIONS (?)

A new calendar is proposed for rangers use which will supercede the obsolete Gregorian Calendar and will more nearly fit the job, as it works out.

Sun	Sun	Mon	Tue	Wed	Thu	Sat
7	6	5	4	3	2	1
14	13	12	11	10	9	8
½	19	18	17	16	15	1
26	25	24	23	22	21	20

The first day of the month is made the seventh day so it is easier to make the deadlines. One can start a report on the seventh and mail it on the first.

With most deadlines coming on the first of the month two are provided giving twice the possibility of being on time.

With yesterday coming two days before tomorrow the rangers will have no trouble with those supervisors who wake up wanting things yesterday.

There are no Fridays since those days are usually wasted in meetings anyway.

Extra Sundays are provided for the overflow of hunters and fishermen and to provide for extra non-office hours for phone calls to your home.

There are only twenty-six days in the month which fits the normal situation of having all the project money spent by that time.

A half day is provided since this was prepared by a half wit.

42. The Equal-Opportunity Christmas Memo

The fight for equal opportunity of employment has had its effect upon urban folklore. The long period of American history in which members of minority groups were simply systematically excluded from particular occupations is at last coming to a close. Unfortunately, prejudice has not disappeared, and it is all too clear that it is difficult, if not impossible, to legislate morality. The following Christmas memorandum contains an implicit criticism of the U.S. government's attempts to suggest quotas for employment of black Americans. While civil-rights legislation has accelerated the integration of many companies and expanded the job opportunities for Negro candidates, it has also resulted in the employment of minority-group individuals just to meet unofficial quotas. Moreover, the whole idea of a quota implies an arbitrary fixed limit. White racists might complain that they were forced to hire x number of black persons, while militant blacks might complain that the establishment of a quota produces a definite upper limit to employment possibilities. While ideally there should not need to be a de facto quota, it is probably true that, without employment goals, there would be no substantial progress in achieving nondiscrimination in employment. The false premise in the Christmas memorandum is that pro-black necessarily means anti-white. If one offers chocolate ice cream, it need not be instead of vanilla. Obviously, both flavors can be offered. Pro-black and pro-white are not mutually exclusive. We find it somewhat ironic that Christmas, a time supposedly devoted to brotherhood and peace on earth, is used to express white resentment at enforced quota integration. On the other hand, in view of the fact that blacks have been forced to worship the principals (and principles) of white Christianity—in an attempt to wash away the "blackness" of sin—it is perfectly appropriate that there is finally black representation among the lily-white angels.

MEMORANDUM

To: All Employees

From: Your Christmas Chairman

We have been informed by the Office of Health, Education and Welfare in Washington that a White Christmas would be in violation of Title 11 of the Civil Rights Act of 1964. Therefore, the following steps are to be taken to insure that we comply with the Act during the Christmas season:

1. All Christmas trees must have at least 23.4% colored bulbs, and they must be placed throughout the tree and not segregated in back of the tree.
2. Christmas presents cannot be wrapped in white paper. However, interim approval can be given if colored ribbon is used to tie them.
3. If a manger scene is used, 20% of the angels and one out of the Three Kings must be of the minority race.
4. If Christmas music is played, "*We Shall Overcome*" must be given equal time. Under no circumstances is "*I'm Dreaming of a White Christmas*" to be played.
5. Care should be taken in party planning. For example:
   (a.) Use pink champagne instead of white.
   (b.) Turkey may be served but only if the white and dark meat are on the same platter. There will be no separate but equal platters permitted.
   (c.) Use chocolate revel ice cream instead of vanilla.
   (d.) Both chocolate and white milk must be served. There will be no freedom of choice plan. Milk will be served without regard to color.

A team from HEW will visit us on December 25th to determine our compliance with the Act. *If it snows on Christmas Eve, we are all in trouble.*

43. The Office Party

In most cultures one or more days in the year are set aside as a time of license, when standard taboos are temporarily suspended. In American offices, such a day occurs on the occasion of the annual (or monthly or even weekly) office party. (Frequently, the annual party is held around Christmas.) At such parties, status distinctions disappear or are often blurred by the extensive consumption of alcoholic beverages. Office-produced tensions are given a much-needed outlet, although sometimes the behavior goes beyond permissible boundaries, even when one considers the relaxed rules in effect for the duration of the party. In such a case, new tensions may arise. A traditional description of the office-party institution goes as follows:

To: Joe P. Maldon and Staff

From: Ex-Employee

Subject: Office Party

When I came into the office this morning, I noticed a sort of general feeling of unfriendliness. Since several of you have openly called me a dirty son-of-a-bitch to my face, I know I must have done something wrong at our office party last Friday. The office manager called me from the hospital, and as this is my last day, I'd like to take this way of apologizing to all of you. I would prefer speaking to everyone personally, but you all seem to go deaf and dumb whenever I try to talk with you.

First, to my dear and beloved boss, Mr. Simons, I am sorry for all the things I called you Friday afternoon. I am very much aware that your father is not a baboon, nor is your mother a Chinese whore. Your wife is a delightful woman and my story of buying her for fifty cents in Tiajuana was simply a figment of my imagination. Your children are undoubtedly yours, too. About the water cooler incident, well, you will never know how badly I feel about it, and I hope they didn't hurt your head when they were trying to get the glass jar off.

To comely Miss Ashley, I express my deepest regrets. In my own defense, I must remind you that you seemed to enjoy our little escapade on the stairway as much as I did until the bannister broke and we fell eight feet to the second floor landing. In spite of the rupture you incurred when I landed on top of you, I am sure you will admit that when we landed, it was one of the biggest thrills you have ever had.

Sam Franklin, you old cuss, you've just got to forgive me for that little prank I played on you. If I had known you were goosey, I would never have done it. It could have been a lot worse if that fat lady hadn't been standing right under the window you jumped through. She broke your fall a lot. People have been killed falling three stories.

Mr. Gray, I regret telling the firemen it was you who turned in the false alarm. But, of course, I had no way of knowing they would be such bad sports about it. Those fire hoses sure have a lot of pressure, don't they? And the water is so cold!

Bill Granfield, you rate a special apology. My laughing when you forgot to put the seat down and got stuck in the john was bad enough, but my calling everyone else into the rest room was unforgivable.

Bill Thompson, I know how you must feel about me opening the door to the mop closet so suddenly. It must have startled you and Miss Finch quite badly. When I think of how hard you bumped your chin on the sink when you bent down to pull up your pants, it makes me sick. We will have to get together for dinner sometime after the dentist finishes your plates.

Miss Brown, the only excuse I can offer for stealing all of your clothes and hiding them when I found you had passed out in the ladies' room is that I was drunk. Also, I want you to know I was very embarrassed when I couldn't remember where I hid them and you had to go home in that old sofa cover. Running your falsies out on the flagpole was a bit too much I guess, but, like I said, I was a bit drunk.

To all the rest of you, I'm sorry. Setting Mrs. Botts' lace panties on fire seemed like a funny idea at the time, but it makes me sad to hear that her husband is getting a divorce because of what I did. Pissing in everyone's drink was in bad taste and not telling them until you all drank them was even worse. Now that I have apologized to all of you, and I know that I'll be forgiven, I've got a surprise for you! Even though I don't work here anymore, I'm going to do my best to get back for the office picnic next Friday.

Your Friend and Ex-Co-Worker

44. The Surprise Party

Not all the parties are meant for the entire office staff. Part of the stereotype of office interpersonal relationships includes the boss's affair with his attractive secretary. The following joke text, xerographically transmitted in written form, plays upon this stereotype.[3] In this case, there is undoubtedly employee pleasure in seeing a "boss" revealed in a compromising position. Note also the moral quality of the "plot." A man who betrays his wife deserves to be betrayed by his secretary. In another form of the surprise party, a bean gourmet is betrayed by his wife.

SURPRISE!

The boss of a medium-sized office had hired a steno who was out of this world. She had looks, personality and clothes. After looking at her for a few weeks, the boss, a married man, decided that he was going to take her out some night. He approached her and asked if she would like to celebrate his birthday with him at some secluded night spot. She said that she would have to think about accepting. The next day she consented to go but offered that they go to her apartment instead of out somewhere. To himself, as any other normal man would, he commented, "better than I planned."

[3]A version of this text appears in J. M. Elgart, ed., *More Over Sexteen* (New York: Grayson Publishing Corp., 1953), p. 50.

The night of his birthday, they went to her apartment and had cocktails, appetizers, dinner and some drinks afterwards. A short while later, she said, "I am going to my bedroom now, and you can come in—in five minutes." After four minutes had gone by the boss started to disrobe. Totally naked by the time five minutes were up, he tapped on the door. The voice from behind the door in a sweet tone said, "come in." A twist of the door knob and the door was open—only to show the rest of the office force singing:

HAPPY BIRTHDAY TO YOU
HAPPY BIRTHDAY TO YOU.

Once upon a time there lived a man who had a maddening passion for baked beans. He loved them but they always had a very embarrassing and somewhat odorous reaction on him. Then one day he met a girl and fell in love. When it was apparent they would marry he thought to himself, she is such a sweet and gentle girl she will never go for this kind of carrying on. So he made the supreme sacrifice and gave up beans. They were married shortly thereafter.

Some months later, his car broke down on the way home from work, and since they lived in the country he called his wife and told her he would be late, because he had to walk home. On his way he passed a small cafe and the odor of freshly baked beans was overwhelming. He had several miles to walk so he figured that the effects of the beans would wear off before he got home, so he stopped at the cafe and had three orders of baked beans. All the way home he putt-putted and after arriving felt reasonably safe that he had putted his last putt. His wife seemed somewhat excited and agitated to see him and exclaimed delightedly, "Darling, I have the most wonderful surprise for dinner tonight." She then blindfolded him and led him to his chair at the head of the table. He seated himself and just as she was ready to remove the blindfold, the telephone rang. She made him vow not to touch the blindfold until she returned, then went to answer the phone.

He seized the opportunity, shifted his weight to one leg and let go. It was not only loud, but as ripe as a rotten egg. He took the napkin and fanned vigorously the air about him. Things had just returned to normal when he felt another urge coming on him, so he shifted his weight to the other leg and let go again. This was a true prize winner. While keeping his ear on the conversation in the hall, he went on like this for about 10 minutes until he knew the phone farewell meant the end of his loneliness and freedom. He placed the napkin on his lap and folded his hands on top of it and smiling contentedly to himself, he was the picture of innocence. When his wife returned, apologizing for taking so long, she asked if he had removed the blindfold. When convinced that he hadn't removed the blindfold, she removed the blindfold, and there sitting around the dining room table were twelve dinner guests for his surprise birthday dinner.

45. The Expense Account

The boss-stenographer romance can also be expressed by other means. In the following unusual narrative form, it is the conventional expense account that tells the story. Once again, there is a moral twist to the item. Sin leads to trouble, and the sacredness of marriage and the home is reaffirmed.

EXPENSE STATEMENT

10/4	Ad for female stenographer	1.00
10/4	Violets for new stenographer	1.50
10/6	Week's salary for new stenographer	45.00
10/9	Roses for stenographer	5.00
10/10	Candy for wife	.90
10/13	Lunch for stenographer	7.00
10/15	Week's salary for stenographer	60.00
10/16	Movie tickets for wife and self	1.20
10/18	Theatre tickets for steno and self	16.00

10/19	Ice cream sundae for wife	.30
10/22	Mary's salary	75.00
10/23	Champagne and dinner for Mary and self	32.50
10/25	Doctor for stupid stenographer	375.00
10/26	Mink Stole for wife	1,700.00
10/27	Ad for male stenographer	1.00

46. The Boss

An elaborate way of characterizing one's boss is by using the following anatomical debate. Curiously enough, this text seems to have a long history. It is almost certainly related to the classical tale of the debate between the belly and other body parts in which the relative usefulness of each part is argued.[4] If this is so, then the office copier in this instance has not created new folklore but simply provided a new outlet for an old form.

THE BOSS

When God made man there was only one. The various parts argued about who would be boss. The *hands* said they should be boss, because they did all the work. The *feet* thought they should be boss, because they took man where he could do the work and get food. The *stomach* thought it should be boss, because it digested the food. The *heart* thought it should be boss, because it pumped the blood that allowed the food to be digested by the stomach. The *brain* said, "I have to send all the signals to get each of you to do your job, therefore I am the boss!" The *asshole*

[4]For further consideration of this folktale, which is found in Aesopic collections among others, see the references listed under Aarne-Thompson tale type 293, Debate of the Belly and the Members, in Stith Thompson, *The Types of the Folktale*, FFC 184 (Helsinki: Academia Scientiarum Fennica, 1961). See also G. Legman's note on the tale in Roger D. Abrahams, *Deep Down in the Jungle* (Hatboro: Folklore Associates, 1964), p. 200. There is also variation in the moral. In the version in the Bible (1 Corinthians 12), for example, all the body parts are equal and mutually dependent.

said, "I'll show you who's boss!" So he closed up and wouldn't let anything pass. After a few days, the stomach ached . . . the hands were practically helpless . . . the feet could not carry the body . . . the heart was about ready to stop pumping blood . . . the brain's signals were being ignored.

TO ALL THIS, THERE IS A MORAL

YOU DON'T HAVE TO BE A *BRAIN* TO BE A BOSS . . . . JUST AN *ASSHOLE*

47. A New Tax

It has become more and more common in American society for the "boss" of an increasing number of employees to be the state or federal government. In any case, all American citizens are subject to regulation by this kind of boss. As government has grown larger, it has required more financial support. This support is normally obtained through taxation. Taxation and taxation regulations have continued to increase in complexity and seem to have pervaded nearly every facet of human activity, which at any rate appears to be the main thrust of the following notice. Of interest also is the stereotyped concern with phallic length as a measure of male status among peers.

STATE OF CALIFORNIA
Franchise Tax Board

Notice of increased tax payment effective 1 July 1969
To: All male taxpayers

Gentlemen:
    The only thing the great State of California has not yet taxed is your Peter, mostly because 98% of the time it is out of work, and the other 2% of the time it is in the hole, because it has two dependents who are nuts.
    However beginning 1 July 1969 your Peter will be taxed ac-

cording to the size. Please check personal size using chart enclosed to determine your category. Please insert this information
on Page 2, Section F, Line O of your State of California Tax
Form.

10 to 12 Inches .... Luxury Tax
8 to 10 Inches .... Pole Tax
6 to 8 Inches .... Privilege Tax
4 to 6 Inches .... Nuisance Tax

Anyone under 4 inches is eligible for a refund. Please do not
request extensions.

Sincerely yours,

Ronald Reagan
Governor

P. S. Any male exceeding 12 Inches —— R.S.V.P.

48. Sell Drinks at Home

With all the anxiety about the high cost of living and the difficulty of providing for one's family, it is reasonable that counsel
should be provided to help individuals beat the system. Another
problem in American society is that of alcoholism. In the following text, the problem drinker is not asked to give up drinking,
but rather to make some profit by indulging in his vice in his
own home. One is tempted to argue that one theme in American
business is to make sin profitable or in any case to convert a lia-
bility into an asset. On the other hand, the puritanical streak pre-
vails insofar as evil must be punished and good must triumph.
The boozer-businessman suffers an early death, leaving his widow to enjoy the fruits of his labor with a "decent" man.

PROFIT   PROFIT
SELL DRINKS AT HOME

If you cannot refrain from leaving half of your pay
check in taverns, why not start a saloon in your own

home? If you are the only customer, you will not have to buy a license.

Give your wife $55 to buy a case of whiskey. There are roughly 240 snorts in a case. Buy all of your drinks from your wife at 60¢ a snort and in twelve days, when the case is gone, your wife will have $89 to put in the bank and you will have $55 left to start up business again. If you live ten years and continue to buy all of your booze from your wife, your widow will have $27,085.47 on deposit . . . enough to bury you respectably, bring up your children, pay off the mortgage on the house . . . marry a decent man and forget she ever knew you!

49. Coho Salmon Experiments in Lake Michigan

The influence of the federal government has gradually become so pervasive that it affects nearly every aspect of the daily lives of all Americans. It is difficult to imagine any activity that does not in theory fall under the official purview of some government agency. The endless stream of reports and memoranda issued by the vast array of government offices deals with a wide variety of subjects. The following text describes the introduction of Coho salmon into Lake Michigan. It has an air of authenticity inasmuch as Coho salmon were actually introduced into the Great Lakes where they flourished much to the delight of local fishermen.

U.S. DEPT. FISH AND GAME
Coho Salmon Experiments in Lake Michigan

The "Coho," not being a native of the Lake Michigan water, has experienced difficulty in surviving. The female, when going up the Lake Michigan feeder streams, has been losing her roe on the rocky stream bottom, and when she got far enough up stream into the small pools and inlets, had great difficulty getting back into the main stream over the sand bars to return to Lake Michigan. In fact as high as 90% were dying at the upper reaches of the Lake Michigan tributaries, which caused an odor problem.

The Michigan sportsmen decided to crossbreed the "COHO" with the native "WALLEYE" for two reasons: (1) The WALLEYE knew Lake Michigan tributaries and, (2) was not so prone to lose the roe while going up stream. Hence, the name "COWAL." This experiment backfired because the fighting "COHO" mixed with the rather sluggish WALLEYE had lost most of the fight the COHO was noted for.

In a further experiment, they bred the "COWAL" with the greatest fresh water fighter in North America, the "MUSKIE," in an effort to make this double crossbreed the top American game fish. They named this hybrid the "COWALSKI!" and now they have to teach the dumb son-of-a-bitch to swim.[5]

50. In Case of Nuclear Bomb Attack

Another notice that gives the appearance of emanating from a government office is concerned with one of the deep-seated anxieties of modern life: the threat of nuclear war. Despite the alleged safety afforded by bomb shelters and the issuance of detailed instructions by Civil Defense authorities, the folk seem to have grave doubts about chances of survival in the event of a nuclear attack.

---

[5]For other examples of this folkloristic tradition, see Alan Dundes, "A Study of Ethnic Slurs: The Jew and the Polack in the United States," *Journal of American Folklore* 84 (1971): 186–203.

NOTICE

OFFICE OF CIVILIAN DEFENSE
WASHINGTON, D. C.

INSTRUCTION TO PATRONS ON PREMISES IN CASE OF NUCLEAR BOMB ATTACK:

UPON THE FIRST WARNING:

1. STAY CLEAR OF ALL WINDOWS.

2. KEEP HANDS FREE OF GLASSES, BOTTLES, CIGARETTES, ETC.

3. STAND AWAY FROM BAR, TABLES, ORCHESTRA, EQUIPMENT AND FURNITURE.

4. LOOSEN NECKTIE, UNBUTTON COAT AND ANY OTHER RESTRICTIVE CLOTHING.

5. REMOVE GLASSES, EMPTY POCKETS OF ALL SHARP OBJECTS SUCH AS PENS, PENCILS, ETC.

6. IMMEDIATELY UPON SEEING THE BRILLIANT FLASH OF NUCLEAR EXPLOSION, BEND OVER AND PLACE YOUR HEAD FIRMLY BETWEEN YOUR LEGS.

7. THEN KISS YOUR ASS GOODBYE.

51. Indoctrination for Soldiers Returning Home

An area that has always been under strict government control is the military. As anyone who has been in the service knows very well, thousands of regulations ensure conformity and compliance to military norms. An individual is not only indoctrinated upon entering the service, but is also instructed on making the transition from military to civilian life upon release from active duty. The following is a fake government notice directed to either the individual soldier or his immediate family or friends. Of course, a real adjustment is required in the process of returning home after military service. The contrast between military and civilian life certainly emphasizes the dehumanizing aspects of the former, especially in time of war.

The first text, dating from 1945, was reported to have circulated among returning troops in Guam. Notice that Americans are described as a "foreign" people; this same kind of writing style is found in the various brief introductory sketches of peoples around the world that are specially prepared for servicemen.

The second version dates from circa 1967 and refers to the Viet Nam war. The specific content in these two versions varies, but the general theme and format are the same.[6]

___

[6]In another version of this second text, dating from 1963, there are numerous indications that it is a traditional text. Whole paragraphs are nearly identical, including the opening and closing ones. For example, the opening sentence in the 1963 text is: "Very soon the above named enlisted man will once again be in your midst, demoralized, devitalized, and defeated." The closing paragraph refers to a "heart of gold" and a "hollow shell of the once proud civilian you once knew him to be."

HEADQUARTERS
9696th Bombardment Wing
APO 334 c/o Postmaster
San Francisco, Calif.   30 June 1945

4110.99

Subject: Indoctrination for Return to U.S.
To: All Units

1. In compliance with current policies for rotation of armed forces overseas, it is directed that, in order to maintain the high standard of character of the American soldier and to prevent any dishonor to reflect on the uniform, all individuals eligible for return to the U.S. under current directives will undergo an indoctrination course of demilitarization prior to approval of his application for return.

2. The following points will be emphasized in the subject indoctrination course:

a. In America there is a remarkable number of beautiful girls. These young girls HAVE NOT been liberated and many are gainfully employed as stenographers, salesgirls and beauty shop operators or welders. Contrary to current practices, they should not be approached with "How Much?" A proper greeting is "Isn't it a lovely day?" or "Have you ever been in Chicago?" Then say, "How Much?"

b. A guest in a private home is usually awakened in the morning by a light tapping on his door and an invitation to join the host at breakfast. It is proper to say "I'll be there shortly." DO NOT say "Blow it out your ———!"

c. A typical American breakfast consists of such strange foods as cantaloupe, fresh eggs, milk, ham, etc. These are highly palatable and though strange in appearance, they are extremely tasty. Butter, made from cream, is often served. If you wish some butter, you turn to the person nearest it and say quietly, "Please pass the butter." You DO NOT say "Throw me the Goddam grease!"

d. Very natural urges are apt to occur when in a crowd. If it is found necessary to defecate, one does not grab a shovel in one hand and paper in the other and run for the garden. At least 90% of American homes have one room called the "Bathroom," i.e., a room that, in most cases, contains a bathtub, wash basin, medicine cabinet, and a toilet. It is the latter that you will use in this case. Instructors should make sure that all personnel understand the operation of a toilet, particularly the lever or button arrangement that serves to prepare the device for re-use.

e. In the event the helmet is retained by the individual, he will refrain from using it as a chair, wash bowl, bathtub, or foot-bath. All these devices are furnished in the average American home. It is not considered good practice to squat Indian-fashion in the corner in the event all chairs are occupied. The host will usually provide suitable seats.

f. Belching or passing wind in company is strictly frowned upon, but if you should forget about it and belch in the presence of others, a proper remark is "Excuse me." DO NOT say "It must be that lousy chow we've been getting."

g. American dinners, in most cases, consist of several items, each served in a separate dish. The common practice of mixing various items, such as corned beef and pudding, or lima beans and peaches, to make it more palatable will be refrained from. In time the "Separate Dish" system will become more enjoyable.

h. Americans have a strange taste for stimulants. The drinks in common usage on this island, such as underripe wine, alcohol and grapefruit juice, or gasoline, bitters, and water, are not ordinarily acceptable in civilian circles. These drinks should be served only to those who are definitely not within the inner circle of friends. A suitable use for such drinks is for serving one's landlord in order to break an undesirable lease.

i. The returning soldier is apt to often find his opinion different from those of his civilian associates. One should call upon his reserve of etiquette and correct his acquaintances with such remarks as "I believe you have made a mistake" or "I am afraid you are in error on that." DO NOT say "Brother, you're really f——d up!"

j. Upon leaving a friend's home after a visit, one may find his hat misplaced. Frequently it has been placed in a closet. One should turn to one's host and say "I don't seem to have my hat. Could you help me find it?" DO NOT say "Don't anybody leave this room; some s.o.b. has stolen my hat!"

k. In traveling in the U.S., particularly in a strange city, it is often necessary to spend the night. Hotels are provided for this purpose and one can get directions to the nearest hotel from anyone. Here, for a small sum one can register and be shown to a room where he can sleep for the night. The present practice of entering the nearest house, throwing the occupants into the yard, and taking over the premises will cease.

l. Whiskey, a common American drink, may be offered to the soldier on social occasions. It is considered a reflection on the uniform to snatch the bottle from the hostess and drain the bottle, cork and all. All individuals are cautioned to exercise extreme control in these circumstances.

m. In motion picture theaters, seats are provided. Helmets are not required. It is not considered good form to whistle every time a female over 8 and under 80 crosses the screen. If vision is impaired by the person in the seat in front, there are plenty of other seats which can be occupied. DO NOT hit him across the back of the head and say "Move your head, Jerk, I can't see a damned thing!"

n. It is not proper to go around hitting everyone of draft age in civilian clothes. He might have been released from the service for medical reasons; ask for his credentials, and if he can't show any, THEN go ahead and slug him.

o. Upon retiring, one will often find a pair of pajamas laid out on the bed. (Pajamas, it should be explained, are two-piece garments which are donned after all clothing has been removed.) The soldier, confronted by these garments, should assume an air of familiarity and act as though he were used to them. Under no circumstances say "How in the hell do you expect me to sleep in a get-up like this?" A casual remark such as "My, what a delicate shade of blue" will usually suffice.

p. Natural functions will continue. It may be necessary frequently to urinate. DO NOT walk behind the nearest tree or automobile you find to accomplish this. Toilets (2.d. above) are provided in all public buildings for this purpose. Signs on some doors will read "LADIES" which literally means "OFF LIMITS TO ALL TROOPS!"

q. Beer is sometimes served in bottles. A cap remover is usually available, and it is not good form to open the bottle by the use of one's teeth.

r. Air raids and enemy patrols are not encountered in America. Therefore, it is not necessary to wear the helmet in church or at social gatherings, or to hold the weapon at ready, loaded and cocked, when talking to civilians in the street.

s. Every American home and all hotels are equipped with bathing facilities. When desired to take a bath, it is not considered good form to find the nearest pool or stream, strip down and indulge in a bath. This particularly is true in the heavily populated areas.

t. All individuals returning to the U.S. will make every effort to conform to the customs and habits of the regions visited to make themselves as inconspicuous as possible. Any actions that reflect upon the uniform will be promptly dealt with.

FOR THE COMMANDING GENERAL:

J. E. BLANK
Colonel, AGD,
Adjutant General

Issued in Solemn Warning

This _____ Day of _____, 19__

Very soon, _____ will once again be in your midst, de-Americanized, demoralized, and dehydrated, but ready once more to take his place as a human being, to engage in life, liberty, and a somewhat delayed pursuit of happiness.

In making your joyous preparation to welcome him back into respectable society, you must make allowances for the crude environment in which he has suffered for the past twelve months. He may be somewhat Asiaticized, suffering from Viet Cong-itis or perhaps too much Ba Moui Ba.

In a relatively short time, his profanity will decrease enough to permit him to associate with mixed groups, and he soon will be speaking a recognizable form of English. Other symptoms may remain, however. He may pad around in sandals and towel and pick at his food suspiciously as though he thought you were trying to poison him. Please be tolerant when he tries to buy everything at half the asking price, slyly offers to sell cigarettes to the postman, and accuses the grocer of putting battery acid in his Coca-Cola . . . and no, your man does not need psychiatric help if he complains that the water in the shower is too hot, or that his bed is too soft, and lacks a mosquito net. Even this shall pass.

Any of the following sights should be avoided, as they can produce a state of advanced catatonic shock: people dancing or squatting, children with toy grenades, black pyjamas, and round-eyed women. Under no circumstances make flattering remarks about exotic Southeast Asia, avoid mention of the benefits of overseas duty, the romantic sound of monsoon rains on the roof, and above all, never mention exotic Oriental girls. The mere reference to any of these subjects may trigger off an awesome display of violence.

For the first few weeks, he may shy away from crowds at such places as theatres, bus stops, traffic lights etc, refuse to enter establishments that do not have wire mesh screens over the windows, and look around frantically for a hole in which to crawl every time he hears a siren. The sound of an automobile or other vehicle backfiring may also have a curious effect on him, such as, for example, panic.

Keep in mind that beneath this tanned and rugged exterior

there beats a heart of pure gold. Treasure this, for it is about the only thing of value he has left. Treat him with kindness, tolerance, and an occasional fifth of good bourbon, and you will soon be able to rehabilitate this hollow shell of the man you once knew.

SEND NO MORE LETTERS TO VIET NAM AFTER _____ FOR HE IS LEAVING THE TROPICS IN _____ DAYS AND HEADING FOR THE LAND OF THE BIG PX.

In Witness whereof the party of the first part has duly executed this warning and set his hand hereunto.

---

52. Notes on Operation of Rotary-Type Lawn Mowers

One of the classic critiques of government notices and bulletins is the communiqué from the Department of Agriculture concerning lawn mowers. The actual problem is obviously not the lawn mower, but how to keep housepets in an urban or suburban environment. With all our super technology, we have not yet solved the problem of disposing of animal waste. Although the problem may strike the uninitiated as trivial, the routine of walking or curbing one's dog has caused innumerable neighborhood squabbles and has no doubt contributed to increasingly widespread enactments of leash laws. Moreover, the primary issue concerns a theme noted previously, the American's aversion to feces. Again the typical American toilet training *for humans* makes Americans project this and other human norms to their household pets. Dogs may have human names, dishes to eat from, meal times at set hours, and so forth. They may even have to learn a doggie equivalent of the human greeting gesture of shaking hands! Cats are trained to use "toilet" litter boxes, while dogs are ordered to use (news)paper. Pets must not only be "housebroken" but should "ask" to go outside, much as a schoolchild learns to raise his hand to ask to be excused. Once outside, the pet is expected to be discreet and not defecate on a sidewalk or main thoroughfare. In cities, fire hydrants usually serve in place of trees, but the poor dog frequently has no convenient place to defecate. As a result, dog feces litter the streets, and Americans squirm at the thought of stepping in excrement or at the prospect of removing feces from their person or property.

Department of Agriculture
Bulletin No. 34709
July, 1954

Notes on Operation of Rotary Type Lawn Mowers

Power driven rotary lawn mowers are a great boon to lazy shiftless suburbanites whose lawns are full of dandelions, buckthorn and other weeds too tall for the reel type, or conventional grass cutters.

The rotary mower, however, is certainly not an unmixed blessing. Unseen rocks and sticks, to say nothing of unburied bones, will raise regular hell with the blades. So will nails, bits of wire and all other metal debris.

But these problems pale into insignificance compared with the unhappy results of running a rotary lawn mower over a new deposit of dog shit. Until you have had your shoes shined with pulverized dog shit, you cannot fully appreciate the extent of the problem.

Cat shit, to be sure, smells worse and is exceedingly messy, but cats, as everyone knows, are more careful to cover up their waste than are dogs. Moreover, cats do not shit as much as dogs, unless you have a very small dog and/or a very large cat.

There are a number of approaches to the problem of animal excreta versus the rotary lawn mower, but unfortunately no real solution. First, of course, you can try to keep dogs (and cats) away from your lawn. The only effective method for doing this is to buy a dog bigger and meaner than any other dog in the neighborhood and train him (a) to chase other dogs off your grass (b) to shit on neighbor's yards. There are obvious drawbacks to this method of combating the problems, however.

First, of course, there is always the chance that one of your neighbors will hire a cow and train it to deposit cow flop on your lawn. It has been reliably estimated that a rotary lawn mower operating at 450 RPM can hurl a normal deposit of cow shit as high as your second story windows and cover an area of 500 square feet. Moreover, if you have an exceedingly high-powered lawn mower and a cow with a big appetite, the results can be disastrous.

Building a fence is a possible solution, but expensive. It is, in addition, no good unless you can train your wife and children to keep the gates shut. And, of course, some dogs will jump fences even if they are full of shit.

There are various commercial preparations, sold mostly to evil-minded old maids, which are supposed to discourage dogs from (a) chasing lady dogs around your house, or (b) watering your shrubs. These chemicals are absolutely worthless since it is second nature for dogs to pursue these pleasures. Even if these preparations did work, of course, they would not solve the basic problem of the rotary lawn mowers. There are, however, four alternatives left for you to take.

1. Let the goddamned weeds grow.
2. Move to a second story apartment and use the mower for a window fan.
3. Wear brown shoes while mowing the lawn and associate with people who either don't mind the smell of shit or are too polite to mention it.
4. Plow under your shrubs and lawn and plant cactus.

Applications and Tests

From the cradle to the grave, modern urban man is subjected to an infinitude of required application forms and tests. One stands in long lines just to obtain an application blank and then in equally long lines to submit the completed form. There are applications for nursery school, for college, for jobs, and for credit; there are tests for licenses and for every level of American education. Filling out forms and taking tests claim an inordinate amount of the average American's time and attention. The impersonality of "form" living is signaled in part by the fact that one is more often than not identified by one's social-security number rather than by one's name.

53. Are You Qualified for a Date with a Paratrooper?

In contrast to most societies of the world where marriages have normally been arranged by adult members of different families, Americans pride themselves upon having the freedom to select their own mates on an individual basis. The custom of "dating" is perhaps a kind of "trial and error" method of mate selection. Yet those individuals who have been unsuccessful in finding a compatible member of the opposite sex need some assistance. Whether it is a lonely-hearts club or a contemporary computerized-dating service, the individual concerned is asked to fill out a personal-history form indicating critical likes and dislikes. The following text is a parody of such application forms. As it is an example of paratrooper folklore, it displays a definite masculine point of view. The male attitude toward dating is *not* necessarily concerned with marriage, but rather with sexual adventures, preferably free from any future obligation. (Note the reference to a family shotgun, referring to the undesirability of a "shotgun" wedding in which an injured girl's family forces the offending male—at gunpoint if necessary—to marry the girl.)

HEADQUARTERS
Second Airborne Battle Group 503D Infantry
Combat Team

Subject: Are You Qualified for a Date with a Paratrooper?

1. Name_____ Address_____
2. City_____ State_____
3. Birthday_____ Flowers preferred_____
4. Favorite song_____ Sport_____
5. Color of hair_____ Eyes_____ Age_____
6. Height_____ Weight_____ Complexion_____
7. Figure: (Check one) Excellent_____ Devine _____ Fair_____
   Oops!____
8. Measurements: Neck_____ Bust_____ Waist_____ Hips_____
   Thigh_____ Knee_____ Calf____ Ankle____
9. Kind of perfume_____ Use it on letters_____
10. Do you drink?_____ How much?_____
11. What is your capacity for the following? Beer_____
    Wine_____ Scotch_____ Whiskey_____ Brandy_____
    Cider_____ Milk_____

12. Do you smoke?____What kind?____Carry your own?____
13. Do you dance?____ How well?_____ Favorite_____
14. Do you cook?____ How well?_____
15. Do you make Whoopee?____ Who with?____ Why?____
_____ Where?_____
16. Do you like to kiss?_____ Type (Check one) Short and sweet____ Passionately____ French_____ Sisterly____
17. Do you think moonlight and love are out of date?_____
18. What are your thoughts on the mention of "Paratroopers"?
_____
19. May I have a date with you when I get home?_____
20. Do you go to bed early?____ Why?_____
21. Are you a prude?_____ Do you know a good thing when you see it?_____
22. Are you open minded and generous?_____
23. Do you like quiet, small, (Two people) parties?_____
24. What is your ring size?_____

The space at left is for lip prints. It is requested that applicants send photo (Full length photo preferred) along with this application. Do not feel that you will be rejected or accepted on looks alone! A well rounded personality is just as important as a well rounded anything else!

25. Type of lipstick (Smearproof, flavored, etc.)_____
26. Does anyone in your family own a shot gun?_____
Other firearms?_____

I, the undersigned, having read the above questions carefully, swear that I have not knowingly falsified any of the answers to said questions and have answered them correctly to the best of my knowledge.

Signature:_____.

This form is designed for the express purpose of choosing highly qualified young ladies to belong to the highly exclusive inner circle of Paratrooper's Sweethearts. We have banded together to protect innocent, young paratroopers from the many fast, loose women roaming the streets of the world.

If you would like to get in tight (real tight) with the world's best (and highest paid) fighting men, fill out this form and return it to the sender. Your application will be highly welcome. Thank you and good luck.

Sender:_____
AIRBORNE! ALL THE WAY!
"THE MIGHTY ROCK!"   503 INFANTRY!

54. Instrument of Surrender

If the preceding text represented the male request for sexual activity, then the following is the female's compliance with the request—although it is compliance on male terms. All the common female defenses and excuses are apparently knowingly waived. The girl is, after all, asked to sign an "instrument" of "surrender." She has to agree to forego any hopes of marriage and to accept the male philosophy of sex for sex's sake. (It is ironic that an "illegal" act is to be made "legal" through a pseudo-document, an obvious sign of the all-pervasiveness of the paperwork empire in American life and thought.)

The attempt of men to dominate women through legal documents is part of a long history in western civilization of the male suppression of women's rights. One need mention only the patriarchal story of creation, in which woman is said to have been produced from man's body, for a clear-cut instance of a male-oriented document denying female power. Modern examples include the legal denial of the right to vote to women. In view of this fairly continuous tradition of male-imposed inequality, it is likely that the following text is circulated by and for males rather than females.

INSTRUMENT OF SURRENDER

THIS CERTIFIES that I, the under-signed, a female about to enjoy sexual intercourse with _____, am above the age of consent, am in my right mind and not under the influence of any drug or narcotic. Neither does he have to use any force, threats or promises, to influence me. I am in no fear of him whatever; do not expect or want to marry him, don't know whether he is married or not, and don't care. I am not asleep or drunk and am entering into this relation with him because I love it and want it just as much as he does, and if I receive the satisfaction I expect, am willing to play an early return engagement.

FURTHERMORE, I agree never to appear as a witness against him or to prosecute him under the Mann White Slave Act.

Signed, before going to bed this_____ day of _____ 19____

By_____

Witness _____

Address _____

_____
Name of cooperator

_____
Phone No.

_____
Date

_____
Hotel

_____
No. of Times

_____
Date to Worry

_____
How Was It?

☐   ☐   ☐
Good   Bad   Oh Well

_____ day of

_____
19____

_____
Notary Public

55. Virtue Test

One important part of the American sexual code has to do with male boasting. According to this code, sexual conquests are sought not only for their own sake, but also to provide men with suitable materials for boasting sessions with their peer group. In college, in preparatory or high school, and even earlier in the educational *cursus honorum*, boys are rated by their peer groups on the basis of their sexual exploits and expertise. An indication of the particular sexual activities that are valued is provided by various versions of a questionnaire parody entitled "Virtue Test" or "Official Purity Test" or the like. It is obviously doubtful whether anyone would answer the questions posed on the test in an honest and truthful fashion. Nevertheless, the questions themselves serve to reveal a good deal about the American male's sexual fantasy life.

This first version circulated at Indiana University in 1939.

VIRTUE TEST

Grade of 85—is an angel

1.	Ever kiss a girl?	−1
2.	French kiss?	−2
3.	Kiss or be kissed below throat?	−6
4.	Tell dirty jokes in a mixed crowd?	−2
5.	Make a girl cry?	−6
6.	Date an intoxicated person?	−3
7.	Date a married person?	−3
8.	Pet from waist up?	−4
9.	Pet from waist down?	−6
10.	Swim nude with a girl?	−4
11.	Neck in prone position?	−5
12.	Go with an engaged person?	−3
13.	Drink intoxicating liquor?	−3
14.	Pick up a strange girl?	−2
15.	Tell girl you loved her when you didn't?	−1
16.	Neck in bathing suit?	−5
17.	Go the limit?	−10
18.	Help girl dress or undress	−4
19.	Go to house of prostitution?	−8

20. Knowingly go out with a fast girl?   −5
21. Buy contraceptives?   −4
22. Get in bed with a girl?   −7
23. See opposite sex in nude?   −3
24. Go to a burlesque?   −1
25. Go to a roadhouse with a girl?   −3

Add the numbers for Yes answers. Subtract from 100. Number on side tells how much to take off if you ever did it willingly or unwillingly.

Clearly, what was risqué in 1939 is not necessarily so in 1974. Alcohol has been largely replaced by marijuana and other drugs. If anyone wished to have dramatic documentation of the changes that have taken place in the United States in the past several decades with respect to sexual mores, one could not ask for a more revealing piece of data than this pseudo-questionnaire.

A second version, entitled "Official Purity Test" and evidently in circulation at Cal Tech (the copy was obtained from the Kinsey Institute for Sex Research at Indiana University), poses questions that go into considerably greater detail.

OFFICIAL PURITY TEST

Formulated by the Student Houses Intellectual, Theological, & Obscenely Naturalistic Youth Organization, Unlimited (S.H.I.T.-O.N.Y.O.U.), with revisions by the Jewman Club of Fleming House, Cal Tech, and further revisions by the Society for the Propagation and Reciprocal Enhancement of Embuggeration (S.P.R.E.E.). Published and distributed by the S.P.R.E.E. Tract Society under Women are Evil Club Research Grant wac-0003-69f.

Directions: Circle each question to which you answer "no." Your Purity Score is the total number of circled numbers. This test is administered under the Honor System.

Have you ever

1. experienced an erection
2.   "   "   "   in the last three months
3.   "   "   "   for more than one hour continuously
4. had a wet dream
5. smoked a cigarette
6. been out on a date
7. stayed out on a date past 4:00 P.M.
8. had dates on each of the 3 days of one weekend
9. kissed a girl
10.   "   "   "   on the neck
11.   "   "   "   while both of you were in a horizontal position
12.   "   "   "   on the first date
13.   "   "   "   in the last 3 months
14. French kissed (tongue kissed)
15. ear frenched a girl (tongued her in the ear)
16. masturbated in the last 3 months
17. masturbated an average of once a week or more during the last 3 months
18. masturbated an average of once a day or more during the last 3 months
19. simulated intercourse with a pillow
20. discussed masturbation with a girl
21. told dirty jokes to, or been told them by, a girl
22. told a woman you loved her when you did not
23. danced with a woman
24. danced cheek to cheek
25. experienced an erection while dancing
26. pinched or patted a girl's buttocks
27. goosed a woman you had never seen before
28. been to a burlesque show
29. read pornographic literature
30. seen a pornographic movie
31. seen a completely nude woman in the flesh
32. necked continuously for more than 15 minutes
33.   "   "   " "   "   2 hours

34. ejaculated while necking
35. been arrested for other than a traffic violation
36. had an alcoholic drink
37. passed out from excessive use of alcohol
38. successfully used alcohol to lower a girl's resistance
39. petted below the shoulders (not your own)
40. gone through the motions of intercourse with a woman while dressed
41. had "lover's knots" (passion cramps)[1]
42. unfastened a girl's brassiere
43. undressed a girl completely
44. been in bed, since you were 12 years old, with a girl whose age differed from yours by not more than 5 years
45. been undressed by a girl satisfying conditions of No. 44
46. gone swimming with a girl in the nude
47. fondled a girl less than 15 years old since you were 15
48.   "   a covered breast of a human being
49.   "   a bare breast of a human being
50.   "   "   "   "   " "   "   "   in the last 3 months
51.   "   the breast of a woman who was unconscious or asleep
52. sucked the nipple of a breast subsequent to your weaning
53.   "   "   "   " "   "   in the last 3 months
54. put your hand under a girl's skirt
55. fingered a vagina
56.   "   "   "   in the last 3 months
57.   "   "   "   on the first date
58. had your bare genitals fondled by a boy or man (other than by yourself or for medical reasons)
59. had your bare genitals fondled by a woman
60. fondled male genitals other than your own
61.   "   "   "   "   "   "   "   in the last year
62. had oral stimulation of your genitals by a woman
63.   "   "   "   "   "   "   "   "   boy or man
64. ejaculated in anyone's mouth

[1]This painful condition is also known as "lover's nuts" or "blue balls."

65. given oral stimulation to the genitals of a woman
66.   "   "   "   " "   "   " " boy or man
67. inserted your penis into the rectum of a woman
68.   "   "   "   "   "   "   " " boy or man
69. done 69 (ask your mother if you don't know the meaning of this)
70. done 69 in the last 3 months
71. had a penis, other than your own, inserted into your rectum
72. simulated intercourse in the valley between a woman's breasts
73. tried to make a girl
74. ejaculated before an impending entry (into a woman)
75. had sexual intercourse
76. had sexual intercourse using a condom (prophylactic or "Trojan")
77. had sexual intercourse during the last 3 months
78.   "   "   " during menstruation
79.   "   "   " in the Student Houses, other school or college dormitories or similar places
80. had sexual intercourse with more than one woman (not necessarily at the same time)
81. had sexual intercourse with five or more women
82.   "   "   " with ten or more women
83.   "   "   " with more than one woman in the same day or night
84. had sexual intercourse 3 or more times in the same day or night
85. had sexual intercourse 10 or more times with the same woman
86. had sexual intercourse with a virgin
87.   "   "   " with a married woman
88.   "   "   " with a prostitute or "call girl"
89.   "   "   "   "   "   " without using a condom
90. had sexual intercourse sitting up or standing
91.   "   "   " in bed

92. ”   ”   ”   in a car
93. ”   ”   ”   dog style
94. ”   ”   ”   continuously for more than 30 min-
    utes
95. had sexual intercourse with a Negro
96. had veneral disease
97. caused a woman to become pregnant
98. committed statutory rape (intercourse with a girl under 18
    years of age)
99. committed incest
100. been watched during intercourse (other than by your sex
    partner)

56. Government Poverty Application

The welfare state is a cause of concern among many middle-
and upper-class American taxpayers. Many of these individuals
sharply criticize what they believe to be unwarranted government giveaways. In their view, it is ridiculously easy for anyone
to qualify for welfare. Furthermore, the whole work-oriented
capitalistic philosophy seems to be threatened if people are allowed to receive money for the mere asking. On the other hand,
it should be pointed out that "getting something for nothing" is
a common element in American ideal values. Moreover, those
same very rich individuals who live from the income of inherited
wealth cannot really be said to be working for their income. Yet
some of these nonworking wealthy are among the most vocifer-
ous critics of the welfare state. The following item was circulat-
ing in the Social Security Office in Glendale, California, in 1966.

GOVERNMENT POVERTY APPLICATION
The "Shorts" Form No. 1039A

Dear Citizen:
This form is being provided for your use if you have reason to

feel you can qualify for a Government Poverty Grant. May we ask that you carefully study the important questions on this sheet and answer them to the best of your ability. If it can be determined that you qualify as a "Povert," then a Government representative will call on you to determine how much money you need.

1. Do you eat as well as your neighbors?   Yes ( )   No ( )
2. Do you know of other people who
   have more than you?   Yes ( )   No ( )
3. Do you need more money to spend?   Yes ( )   No ( )
4. Do you find it tough to pay your bills? Yes ( )   No ( )
5. Do you know of any reason why you
   should not qualify for a poverty grant? Yes ( )   No ( )

   Please sign (or place your "X") in space below.

Name _____

(only one per applicant)

In order to assist you with the above questions and to help you qualify for a poverty grant, we submit the following suggestions: The answer to question #1 should be "No";
   "   "   "   "   #2   "   " "Yes";
   "   "   "   "   #3   "   " "Yes";
   "   "   "   "   #4   "   " "Yes";
   "   "   "   "   #5   "   " "No".

BONUS OFFER: Do you know of three friends whom you think can qualify for a poverty grant? If so, please send their names and when these people qualify, we will send you another $1,000 POVERTY BONUS.

POVERTY MEANS PROSPERITY Mail your application to the Bureau of Public Health Education and Welfare (PHEW)! BE SOMEBODY! BE A POVERT!

57. Application for Membership in the N.A.A.C.P.

Like it or not, racism is an important current in American life. It is difficult to discuss inasmuch as the very discussion might unwittingly aid the cause of racism. The following text in which the white stereotype of blacks is spelled out will surely be offensive to many readers. Nevertheless, it is part of the American urban folklore—from the North as well as the South—and to the extent that there are racists one would expect to find folklore reflecting racist views. Any view, be it racist or otherwise, when expressed in extreme caricature form may be humorous. Humor comes from tragedy and from pain. Laughing at tragedy helps make tragedy bearable. In this light, one might argue that the presentation of a racist parody is ultimately antiracist. By itemizing all the traits of the stereotype, one demonstrates the absurdity of that stereotype.

APPLICATION FOR MEMBERSHIP IN THE N.A.A.C.P.

Name _____ Date _____
        (Use All Names You Has Gone By)
Address _____
        (If You Live in Automobile, Give Address of Loan Co.
                        and Car Tag No.)
Place of Birth (Check One)
        Charity Hospital _____ Unknown_____
        Public Hospital (Free) _____
        Cotton Field _____
Name of Mother _____
Name of Father (If Known) _____
Marital Status:
        Common Law _____ Hedge Hopper _____
        Fielder's Choice _____ Eunuch _____
        Not of Age (Check if 9 Yrs. Old or Younger) _____

Number of Legitimate Children if Any _____
Number of Children Fathered (If Known) _____
Number of Children Claimed for Welfare Check _____
List of White Schools You Would Like to Attend
    (Use Back of Paper if More Space Needed)
1.   3.   5.   7.   9.
2.   4.   6.   8.   10.
Make of Automobile (Check One) Lincoln _____
    Cadillac_____ Imperial_____
Abilities (Check One)
    Govt. Employee_____ Preacher_____ Agitater_____
    Church Worker_____ Have Razor, Will Travel_____
Give Approximate Income: From Relief_____
    From Theft_____ If Income from Other Source,
    Explain _____
Previous Work Experience: Drawed Unemployment_____
    Idler_____ Greyhound Bus (Passenger)_____
    Allergic to Work_____
Can You Give as References Any of the Following?
    Earl Warren_____ Eleanor Roosevelt_____
    Martin Luther King_____ J. Kasper_____
    RF or JF Kennedy_____
Would You Be Willing to Serve as Director of the
    Ford Foundation_____ Urban League_____
    Attorney General_____ Ambassador to Congo_____

THE PLEDGE

I believes in equality that niggers is better than white folks is, and that white folks should pay more taxes than us niggers should, and us niggers should enjoy more welfare. I is against radical changes in the laws now that us has the Supreme Court and the U.S. Army on our side. I believes in and wants integration, transportation, education, mastication, hibernation, propagation, and donations. And I further pledges to pay any Association dues out of the first welfare check each month.

THE MOTTO:
Floribas pro nil (literal translation—Everything for nothing)

I Know My Rights _____

(Signature)

58. Applicazionne to Joina de Mafia

Folk stereotypes may include a wide variety of alleged characterological traits. The stereotype of the Italian-American, for example, often makes reference to food preferences and clothing styles, not to mention such slurring attributes as stupidity and cowardice (see the Folk Cartoon section of this volume).

One of the most striking facets of the Italian-American stereotype concerns the famous or infamous international organization, presumably originating in Sicily, called the Mafia. With the help of extensive coverage in the mass media, the image of the Mafia has been widely disseminated in the United States and elsewhere. Many Italian-Americans bitterly resent this Mafia image, particularly insofar as the image is perceived as an insulting travesty of the truly positive contributions made by Americans of Italian descent.

The folk image of the Mafia as depicted in the following application form is also of interest because of its feigned attempt to imitate the Italian-American pronunciation of English. The speech pattern presented, of course, may well reveal more about the way non–Italian-Americans *think* Italian-Americans speak than about the way Italian-Americans actually speak. Nevertheless, it is true that there are predictable difficulties that native speakers of Italian are almost bound to encounter when they speak English. (For example, the absence of voiced or voiceless "th" in Italian may account in part for the frequent substitution of "d" for "th" in such words as "with" and "other.")

Traditional behavior associated with organized crime include

the arrangement of assassinations (by putting out a "contract"
and employing a "hit" man), loan-sharking, and prostitution.
There are allusions to all these in this example of urban folklore.

APPLICAZIONNE TO JOINA DE MAFIA

Whazza U Name_____ U-Hage_____
Whassa U Howsa Nummer_____U-Street_____
Whazza U Bag? (If uzza Girl, Oh-Boy!)_____
Justta checka wun. (Wiazza Guy!)
Hitta Man_____ Lona-Arranger_____ Prostitutta_____
Putta downna werea U worgga now _____
Waza U inna de "Bigga Ouse"? _____
For whattza wazza U inna de "Big Ouse"?_____
   I shoote wun guize_____ I keedenappa sumbody's_____
   Proteckshun raggett_____ Udda thingza_____
U wanna b de *Bigga Shotz*, Sumdaze? Yasse___ No___ Eh!___
U likka eat garlic?_____ Pizza_____ Salami_____
U no ow 2 makke de Cement Shooz? _____
U driva de car?___ Cadillac___ Buick_____ Linken_____
U likka Spaghett?___ Galamari___ Gilze___ Boyze___
   (peeka just one—no fool around cus I slappa U face!)
U see de Godfather?_____ (Or justa de movie?)

Widda U entry, U gonna get sometink U reely gonna like
   1 pr. darke glasses
   1 blacke shirte widda wite tie
   1 pr. pointe shooz
   1 pr. "Cement Shooz" (Come later, when U follarounde!)
   1 Appy Face Button
   1 lb. mozzarella cheese
   1 kiss (Come later, onna U cheek!)
   1 wite hat, widda blacke brim
   1 spumoni (tutti-frutti)
   8 x 10 picchur—Frank Sinatra

Good stoff, Eh!? If Ua no like, I tell U what U gonna get!
(Wiazza Guy!)
JOINA DE CLUB NOW ! ! ! ! ! ! ! (While U Still canna write)
G U I S E P P I

The Mafia has always been known for its highly patterned hierarchal organization, which demanded unquestioned loyalty at all levels. Within recent times, it has been rumored that the Mafia has attempted to move from outright criminal acts into more respectable business enterprises. Part of the popular image of big business in the United States (as being ruthless, greedy, and dishonest) makes it easy for Americans to imagine the Mafia operating under the guise of a conventional business. In effect, the business version of the Mafia may be partly a reflection of popular attitudes toward big business in general. Still, some of the details of the following financial statement do refer rather specifically to supposed activities of the Mafia.

MAFIACO
INCORPORATED

FINANCIAL STATEMENT—FISCAL YEAR 1968

INCOME BEFORE TAXES ....$ 12,789,568,598.04
INCOME AFTER TAXES 12,789,568,598.04
ADJUSTED NET INCOME 12,789,568,598.04

ASSETS
  Cash and Securities
    Buried in cellars, etc. ....$ 47,368,537,907.98
    Deposited in Swiss Bank Accounts, etc. 8,638,209,448.11
    Invested in Sicilian Savings Bonds 700,000,000.00
    Stashed in Bus and Railroad Terminal Lockers 3,860,389,680.67
  Accounts Receivable
    Short Term Notes 126,578,790.50
    Interest Due On Short Term Notes 29,589,477,202.29
  Inventories
    Contracts and Work in Progress 589,700,000.00

Equipment

Bullet-Proof Cadillacs and Lincolns	2,863,985.17
Tanks and Armored Cars, etc.	1,685,389.54
Guns and Ammunition	58,806,276.49
Brass Knuckles, Black Jacks and Other Weapons	388,974.39
	90,936,637,655.14

Less Depreciation for Obsolescence

(238,589 Double-Breasted Striped Suits)	417,685.25
	90,936,219,969.89

Properties and Other Interests

Las Vegas	127,568,778,622.03
Miami Beach	70,433,889,457.86
Hoboken	1,687,742.59
Sands Point	980,066.23
Grosse Point	6,299,754.01
Salerno (122,689,500,000 lire)	1,022.00
TOTAL ASSETS $288,947,856,634.61	

LIABILITIES

Wages and Salaries

Executives	150,000,000,000.00
Executives' Wives	81,000,000,000.00
Executives' Relatives	47,000,000,000.00
Executives' Relatives' Wives	9,000,000,000.00
Employees	890,000.00

Expenses

Payoffs To Law Enforcement Officers	927,908,567.00
Payoffs To Government Officials and Judges	69,865,427.00
Funeral Costs	12,680,287.21
Dental Bills For Show Biz Personalities We Own..	72,684.00
Auditors Fee*	439,669.40
TOTAL LIABILITIES $288,947,856,634.61	

AUDITOR'S REPORT TO STOCKHOLDERS
* We have examined the books and financial statements of MAFIA-
CO and in our opinion it represents fairly the results of its operations and the financial position of MAFIACO for the fiscal year of
1968, and anybody don't like it gets his.

(signed)

Alfonso "Big Fish" Baccala
President, Baccala and Baccala
Certified Public Accountants

59. Can You Follow Directions?

In American education, great emphasis is placed upon the ability to follow directions. Even intelligence or aptitude tests sometimes seem to be more concerned with directions than with substantive matter. The following test illustrates the importance of following directions to the letter and the dangers that may result in disregarding or anticipating what is to be done. The implicit educational aim seems to be to encourage children to follow instructions blindly and not to question an order. No doubt it is the introduction of such tests into American educational institutions that readies much of our citizenry to follow orders, no matter how illogical these orders may appear. The goal is, thus, not the exercise of creativity but of following directions. The present test, however, does suggest the folly of unquestioning obedience to any set of sequential orders.

HOWARD RESEARCH TESTING SERVICE
3 Minute Time Test

Can You Follow Directions?

1. Read everything before doing anything.
2. Put your name in the upper right hand corner of this paper.
3. Circle the word "Name" in sentence two.
4. Draw five small squares in the upper left hand corner of this paper.
5. Put an "X" in each square.
7. Sign your name under the title of this paper.
8. After the title, write "Yes," "Yes," "Yes."
9. Put a circle around sentence number seven.
10. Put an "X" in the lower left hand corner of this paper.
11. Draw a triangle around the "X" you just put down.
12. On the back side of this paper, multiply 703 by 66.
13. Draw a rectangle around the word "paper" in sentence number four.

14. Loudly call out your first name when you get to this point in the test.
15. If you think you have followed directions carefully to this point, call out "I Have."
16. On the reverse side of this paper add 8950 and 9850.
17. Put a circle around your answer, and put a square around the circle.
18. Count out in your normal speaking voice, from ten to one backwards.
19. Punch three small holes in the top of this paper with your pencil.
20. If you are the first person to get this far, call out loudly, "I Am the First Person to This Point and I Am the Leader in Following Directions."
21. Underline all even numbers on the side of this page.
22. Put a square around every number which is written out on this page.
23. Say out loud, "I Am Nearly Finished, I Have Followed Directions."
24. Now that you have finished reading carefully, do Only Sentence Two.

The following shorter version depends upon the same basic premise as the preceding one, with several additional details of interest. First of all, one is really asked to do nothing, but the request is effectively concealed. Second, even the carrying out of (un)necessary mechanical operations is to be limited to a specific, confining box on the survey sheet. The phrase "Do your work in this space" is symptomatic of the whole ruinous effect urban life (as opposed to rural) has had on the individual. One resides and works in little boxes! Finally, the overall confusion and irrationality of the form are signaled by the pretentious title and the form identification symbols at the bottom.

ETHNOGRAPHIC DEMOSCOPY DIVISION
King Surveys, Inc.

EXTENDED FAMILIES SURVEY

1. Read all directions before doing anything.
2. Write your name in the upper right-hand corner of this page.
3. Write your age in years in this space: _____
4. Divide this number by the number of persons in your immediate family, i.e., father, mother, brother(s) and/or sister(s). Include step-, half- and adopted relations.

DO YOUR WORK IN THIS SPACE

5. Add to the quotient of #4 (above) the total number of your grandparents still living, WHETHER THEY LIVE IN THE SAME HOUSE WITH YOU OR NOT.

DO YOUR WORK IN THIS SPACE

6. If the result of the foregoing is greater than seven (7), turn this page over on your desk and raise your hand. If it is less than seven (7), stick your right index finger in corresponding ear. If it is exactly seven (7), then draw a picture of a fish.

DO YOUR WORK IN THIS SPACE

7. Now go back and read the first direction. Then stop.

THANK YOU

Obfuscation Form IWNEOFAP-67
LIMDIS: A thru G (QTYDESREQ)

60. Now Your Town Can Have a Professional Riot

The following form is not strictly speaking an application or a test. It is perhaps more an order blank than anything else. Once again, we find an expression of anxiety about an essential feature of American culture, namely, the right of dissent. Strikes and demonstrations have been a part of the American scene ever since the country was founded. (The Boston Tea Party in 1773 is an obvious example.) Certainly, the rise of American labor unions cannot be considered apart from the history of such activities. In recent years, college communities have emerged from idealistic ivory-tower isolation and intellectual passivity or neutrality to play an increasing role in attempting to effect social change. College students, perhaps influenced by a mass media that makes it impossible to remain unaware of critical issues, have demanded that their education be relevant to these issues. Whether the cause is civil rights or opposition to war, students are involved.

Parents and the general public find it difficult to understand the nature of this radical change in the role of colleges and universities, and they tend to underestimate the sincerity of college students. "Demonstrations" are called "riots," and a conspiratorial view of history is invoked to "ensure" that all such disruptive activities can be said to be communist-inspired. In the following text, we find the public's stereotype of college demonstrations neatly encapsulated.

61. University of California Curriculum

The content of university courses has been altered in an attempt to make such courses relevant to the fundamental issues of contemporary life; but the general public's conception of the courses offered is based in part upon the image of the university presented by newspapers, radio, and television. The image is not an intellectual one and, essentially, the extracurricular is depicted as curricular. The following curriculum design reveals not only what the public thinks university students do, but also what they do *not* do (with a strong implication via time allocations that what is supposedly being neglected, for example, personal hygiene, democracy, etc., should be receiving more attention). Although this text dates from 1965 and has specific reference to the University of California, we suspect the attitudes and stereotypes expressed reflect a large segment of American public opinion about what is happening in colleges and universities in all parts of the United States.

1965–1966
UNIVERSITY OF CALIFORNIA CURRICULUM

Freshman Year

1st Semester		*2nd Semester*	
1. Riot 101	4 hrs.	1. Dirty Books 101	3 hrs.
2. Insurrection 121	3 hrs.	2. Russian 102	3 hrs.
3. Russian 101	3 hrs.	3. Insurrection 122	3 hrs.
4. Lab (Riot Technique)	½ hr.	4. Lab (Mob Rule)	½ hr.
5. Political Science 101	3 hrs.	5. Arson Techniques 101	3 hrs.
		6. Arson Lab	2 hrs.
	13½ hrs.		14½ hrs.

Sophomore

1. Personal Hygiene
   (Optional) ....2 Min.
2. Draft Dodging .... 5 hrs.
3. Troop Train
   Delaying ....3 hrs.
4. Lab (Draft Card
   Burning, Train
   Track Lying) ......1 hr.
5. English Composition
   (Picket Signs) 110A .3 hrs.

   ――――――――――
   12 hrs., 2 min.

1. Democracy ....2 Min.
2. Communism ......5 hrs.
3. Civil Disobedience ..3 hrs.
4. O.D. Lab (Sitting,
   Lying & Sleeping In) .1 hr.
5. Composition (4-Let-
   ter Words) 110B ...3 hrs.

   ――――――――――
   12 hrs., 2 min.

Junior

1. Introduction to Free
   Love ....5 hrs.
2. Police Car
   Sit-in 331 ....2 hrs.
3. Car Burning Lab .. ½ hr.
4. Beard Growing 311 ...4 hrs.
5. "Pad" Fabrication
   300 ....2 hrs.

   ――――――――――
   13½ hrs.

1. Sandal Mending 302 .4 hrs.
2. Sweatshirt Washing .. 1 Min.
3. Barber School ......1 Min.
4. Public Speaking .... 3 hrs.
5. Public Speaking
   Lab (Yelling &
   Shouting) ....1 hr.
6. Rules & Regulations
   for understanding
   Welfare & Unemploy-
   ment Collection ....4 hrs.

   ――――――――――
   12 hrs., 2 min.

Senior

1. Job Corps. Prep. .... 6 hrs.
2. Seminar (On-the-Job
   Training for Riots) ..6 hrs.

   ――――――――――
   12 hrs.

1. Seminar on Peaceful
   Demonstration (in-
   cludes 1 Hr. Lab on
   care and handling
   of deadly weapons) ..6 hrs.

2. Seminar on Disrespect
   for Law & Order . . . . 6 hrs.
                            ―――――――
                            12 hrs.

62. My Child Was Absent from School Because . . .

Not only application forms but also the content of applications and other forms have inspired urban folklore. A popular example of (type)written folklore consists of "sentences" supposedly taken at random from allegedly actual application forms or letters. Typical is the list of excuses offered by parents explaining their children's absences from school. Note that the misspellings provide part of the humor and that this humor would be lost if the item were transmitted orally.

Some excuses received by the attendance office of a nearby high school via notes from parents.

Dear school: Pleas exkuse John for being absent on January 28, 29, 30, 31, 32 and 33.

Chris have an acre in his side.

Mary could not come to school because she was bother by very close veins.

John has been absent because he had two teeth taken out of his face.

I kape Billie home because she had to Christmas shopping because I didn't no what size she wear.

John was absent yesterday because he had a stomach.

Please excuse Gloria, She been sick and under the doctor.

My son is under the doctor's care and could not take P.E. Please execute him.

Lillie was absent from school yesterday as she had a gang over.

Please excuse Blanch from P.E. for a few days. Yesterday she fell out of a tree and misplaced her hip.

Please excuse Joyce from jim today. She is administrating.

Please excuse Joey Friday, he had loose vowels.

Carlos was absent yesterday because he was playing football, he was hurt in the growing part.

My daughter wouldn't come to school Monday because she was tired. She spent the weekend with some Marines.

Please excuse Sandra from being absent yesterday. She was in bed with gramps.

Ralph was absent yesterday because of a sour trout [sore throat].

Please excuse Wayne for being out yesterday because he had the fuel.

63. From Applications for Welfare

Similar in content and style to the preceding text is the following superb exemplar of urban folklore. The fact that one is forced to reveal so much of one's private life in order to qualify for welfare payments is a commentary upon the nature of the interaction between the individual and various bureaucracies. It is significant that the letters are all represented as being written by women. Apparently, women are forced to take the initiative in applying for welfare support.

Sentences Taken from Actual Letters by the Welfare Department from Applicants for Aid

1. I am forwarding my marriage certificate and 6 children. I had 7 but one died, which was baptized on a half sheet of paper.

2. I am writing to the welfare department to say that my baby was born 2 years old. When do I get my money?

3. Mrs. Jones has not had any clothes for a year and has been visited regularly by the clergy.

4. I cannot get sick pay. I have 6 children. Can you tell me why?

5. I am glad to report that my husband who was reported missing is dead.

6. This is my eighth child, what are you going to do about it?

7. Please find for certain if my husband is dead; the man I am now living with can't eat or do anything until he knows.

8. I am very much annoyed to find that you have branded my boy illiterate as this is a dirty lie. I was married to his father a week before he was born.

9. In answer to your letter, I have given birth to a boy weighing 10 pounds. I hope this is satisfactory.

10. I am forwarding my marriage certificate and my 3 children, one of which was a mistake, as you will see.

11. My husband got his project cut off 1 week ago and I haven't had any relief since.[2]

12. Unless I get my husband's money soon, I will be forced to lead an immortal life.

13. You have changed my little boy to a girl. Will this make any difference?

[2] G. Legman in his "Rationale of the Dirty Joke," *Neurotica* 9 (1951): 53, remarks that the line "Dere Mr. President: I ain't had no relief since my husband's project was cut off" was included in "funny letters" circulated since the 1930's and included in collections by Juliet Lowell. Lowell has compiled a number of books of letters, e.g., *Dear Sir* (New York: Duell, Sloan, and Pearce, 1944) and *Dear Mr. Congressman* (New York: Duell, Sloan, and Pearce, 1960), but most of the letters are not traditional. Rather they are humorous letters authored by individuals.

14. I have no children yet, as my husband is a bus driver and works day and night.

15. In accordance with your instructions, I have given birth to twins in the enclosed envelope.

16. I want my money as soon as I can get it. I have been in bed with the doctor for 2 months and he doesn't do me any good. If things don't improve, I will have to send for another doctor.

Folk Cartoons and Drawings

Some of the materials presented thus far may have had purely oral antecedents. Such was the case, for example, with the dialogue between the parts of the body. Cartoons and drawings do not have a similar oral source, although, to be sure, many folk cartoons use items of folk speech as a point of departure. To our knowledge, folklorists have not recognized, much less discussed, the existence of traditional cartoons. These cartoons have presumably been popular for many years, but, in the absence of systematic collecting by folklorists, it is difficult to provide a historical perspective for this genre. The office copier has, without doubt, encouraged the creation and diffusion of folk cartoons.

One may legitimately ask how it is possible to demonstrate that a given cartoon is a folk cartoon rather than one of the many cartoons created by professional cartoonists. The answer is based on the same criteria used in the identification of any item of folklore. The item must have "multiple existence," that is, it must exist in more than one time or place or both. Moreover, variation almost always occurs. Two versions of the same folk item are rarely, if ever, exactly identical.

The multiple-existence criterion, plus variation, explains how a cartoon that might have been created originally by a professional cartoonist could pass into folk tradition. Of course, it wouldn't pass into folk tradition unless it caught the imagination of the folk. One additional reason why some of the cartoons presented here are probably folk is their obscene character. It is doubtful whether, until recently, some of them would have appeared in print in the United States.

The criterion of variation is a crucial one in the case of folk cartoons. Frankly, one would think that the office copier might have stifled variation and that a given cartoon would be copied again and again with little or no change. This is simply not the case. The fact that no two versions of a folk cartoon are exactly the same proves conclusively that we are dealing with a true folk form.

64. You'll Always Get Your Reward

Many folk cartoons are based upon the literal representation of a metaphor. Thus, the picture of a man with a screw piercing his midsection is a literal drawing of the phrase "to be screwed" by someone, usually by someone in a position of authority. The caption presents a statement from ideal culture, but the cartoon indicates that hard work is not always properly rewarded. The boss or the company can screw the hardworking employee just as easily as the idler.

The cartoon also reinforces the sexual attributes of the image. "To screw" is slang for having sexual intercourse. Yet, like many other slang terms for intercourse, the nonbiological, figurative usage inevitably possesses a negative connotation rather than a pleasurable one.[1] "To be screwed," "to get fucked," and "to get the shaft" are all illustrations. The male role in intercourse is

[1]On this point see Edward Sagarin, *The Anatomy of Dirty Words* (New York: Lyle Stuart, 1962).

considered to be the dominant one, while the female role is deemed inferior and subordinate. Thus, if one is screwed in the sense of being the passive recipient of the phallic screw, one is not a man but a woman. In the cartoon, the victim is a male, but he is a rather benighted creature and not very masculine. The fact that the screw protrudes from the victim's back indicates that the "penetration" has been a thorough one. The fact that the screw has entered the victim from the front further feminizes him. Had it entered from the back, the implication might have been that the boss was a homosexual or that he had surreptitiously attacked the victim from the rear. By attacking from the front, the boss confirms his own masculinity and at the same time creates a hole in the victim's midsection.

In the various versions of this cartoon, variations occur both in the caption and in the actual drawing. Numerous versions suggest that this is a particularly popular cartoon. (The earliest version we could locate was one published in 1951.)[2] Readers are invited to compare such details as the character's hair style, legs, feet, the screw design, and so on. From the differences, we can only assume that the cartoon has been repeatedly redrawn. Certainly, it would have been a simple matter to machine copy an exact facsimile of an "original" cartoon. Apparently, many of the links in the human transmission chain elect to redraw the character, preserving his general shape and expression, but altering some of the details. Just as each teller of a folktale or joke in some sense makes that story his own, so it would seem that the recreator of a folk cartoon makes a point of placing his personal mark on the tradition.

---

[2]The version in J. M. Elgart, ed., *Over Sexteen* (New York: Elgart Publishing, 1951), p. 73, has the caption "Well how'd you make out with the old man?"

BE GOOD, LOYAL AND WORK HARD
AND YOU WILL GET YOUR JUST REWARD !!!

BE A HARD WORKER
  BE LOYAL AND TRUE
    BE KIND AND GOOD NATURED

YOU'LL ALWAYS GET YOUR REWARD!

BE KIND AND GOOD NATURED YOU'LL ALWAYS GET YOUR REWARD!

BE KIND AND GOOD NATURED
YOU'LL ALWAYS GET YOUR
REWARD!!!

BE KIND AND GOOD-NATURED
AND YOU'LL ALWAYS GET YOUR
REWARD ....

65. The Finger

The following folk cartoon depends upon gestures rather than upon folk speech. One gesture is the familiar "thumbs down," indicating death in the Roman gladiatorial context or simply a strong negative vote in everyday usage. The other gesture, perhaps the single most common gesture in the United States, carries the meaning "Fuck you!" The gesture is variously titled "the finger" (as in "giving someone the finger" and "up yours" or "up your ass"), "the bird" (as used in the locution "flipping the bird"), or less commonly "the freeway sign" (referring to the gesture's utilization on the freeway just after one car has cut suddenly—and often dangerously—in front of another. Either driver may direct the gesture at the other).[3]

The first version was dated 1962. The second version was dated 1966. There appears to be a common tradition, at least judging from details like the broken sword. In any case, the gestures might be said to represent the polarities of life and death. Thumbs down means death, but an erect phallus means life!

---

[3]Several of these titles, e.g., "the bird," are not listed in Harold Wentworth and Stuart Berg Flexner, *Dictionary of American Slang* (New York: Thomas Y. Crowell, 1967). Certainly, "flipping the bird" is widely known in California.

66. Am I People?

The following text depends upon folk speech, specifically the play on the word "laid" and the word "chicken." It appears that we have basically an oral joke that has been translated into a comic strip or cartoon series. The joke could be told without pictures and would still be effective. (One remembers that the "Types of Girls in the Powder Room" discussed earlier occurred both with and without accompanying illustrations. In such instances, the drawings are evidently an optional rather than an obligatory feature.) On the other hand, the existence of variants in the illustrations suggests that the cartoon aspects are in fact traditional and perhaps even essential for maximum aesthetic effect.

A second version bears the interesting title "Facts of Life." It may be that it is poking fun at the middle-class American morality that insists, or at least has insisted, upon euphemisms in discussions of sex education between parents and children. Human sexuality is often referred to as the "Facts of Life" or the "Birds and the Bees." Children upon first asking legitimate questions about such matters are still often handed a book about birds or frogs or the like. One would imagine that a bright child might ask such a parent, "Am I a bird?" or "Am I a bee?" (or "Was I brought by the stork?"). The cartoon sequence reverses this euphemistic tradition inasmuch as the baby chick asks if he is people. But in this folk cartoon appear the characteristic honesty and forthrightness of folklore. The adult chicken, though speaking in poultry terms, makes direct reference to human sexuality and appears to argue in favor of sexual intercourse.

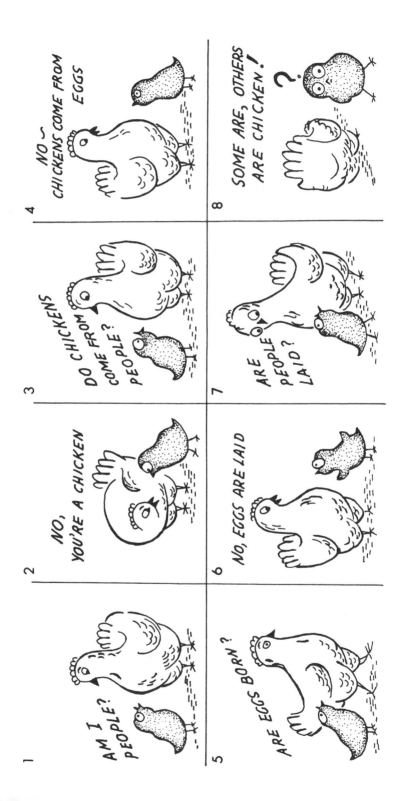

FACTS OF LIFE

67. The Job Is Never Finished Till the Paper Work Is Done

The popular protest against paperwork is surely one of the underlying factors leading to the creation and dissemination of the urban American folklore found in offices around the country. No business deal is concluded until the final contract is signed. Office life is filled with a never-ending flow of preliminary reports, memoranda, surveys, and final evaluations. Yet, as the paperwork empire has created anxiety, it has also provided the medium for a release from that anxiety. Urban folklore transmitted by the office copier is a defense mechanism against almost everything else reproduced in the office routine. In the following folk cartoon, the necessity for paperwork is directly acknowledged, but the text also makes clear that paperwork is unpleasant and unclean. The real effort is made prior to the paperwork, but business requires that loose ends be tidied up so that the deal can be closed. A paperwork trail must be laid or a file built in order to protect the individuals concerned. Many employees and technicians tend to regard paperwork as being somehow less important than the "real" work accomplished by invention and production. For this reason, they view as officious bureaucrats those who enforce the requirement for producing paperwork. The motto of the paperwork empire serves as the caption for the first of the following folk cartoons.

A second version has a slightly different wording of the motto but a similar outhouse. In the third version, the motto remains stable, but the drawing makes more explicit what was previously implicit, perhaps because of a desire to modernize the image. Indoor plumbing has largely replaced the older outhouse, and it is, after all, modern business that has multiplied the amount of required paperwork. A fourth version shows a child rather than an adult.

"THE JOB IS NEVER FINISHED
TILL THE PAPER WORK IS DONE!"

Remember... You're Not Finished Until You've done The Paper Work!

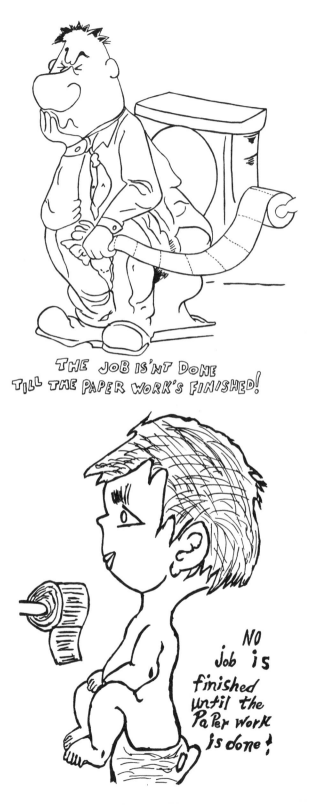

68. The Organization Chart

An especially interesting cartoon reflecting the hierarchical structure of most organizations is the following depiction of several customary gestures. The custom of kissing hands is associated primarily with male-female etiquette in aristocratic circles. It represents gentility. On the other hand, kissing someone's foot, like licking someone's boot, connotes an extreme subordinate-superordinate relationship. Foot-kissing represents exaggerated servility. Finally, the pretended gesture of ass-kissing suggests the most loathsome and fawning behavior of all. Bootlicking and ass-kissing as a means for getting ahead are common enough. Sometimes, the references are somewhat euphemistic. One speaks, for example, of earning "brownie points." But what are they? One gets them from "brown-nosing," not from belonging to the Brownie Scouts and doing good deeds. One gets a brown nose from the act of kissing a superior's ass.

The folk cartoon suggests that the degree of servility depends upon one's position in the power structure: hand-kissing at the top, bootlicking in the middle, and ass-kissing at the bottom. Despite the sins involved in achieving the pinnacle of success, the top man can do no wrong, as signaled by the halo. The fact that he alone does not have to wear matching clothes suggests that he is free from the normal constraints of conformity.

Although the preceding cartoon often occurs by itself as an independent item, in one instance it was accompanied by a second drawing. The second drawing constitutes the delineation of American business-corporation structure, but it does so by depicting heaven in these terms. This drawing has many implications. For one thing, it is true that the Catholic Church does possess considerable hierarchical organization—though admittedly not that illustrated in the drawing. Critics of the Church have even argued that it has operated as a business in the sense of buying and selling property and the like.

The drawing is interesting in that it supports the general notion—common among all peoples of the world—of some kind of correlation between the nature of the afterworld and the nature of life on earth. Sometimes, the relationship is one of opposites: for instance, life is hard on earth and easy in heaven. Sometimes the relationship is one of parallels or even continuities: life in the next world is more or less a direct translation of life in this world. But, in either case, the two worlds show remarkable structural similarities.

The idea that the organization of heaven reflects the organization of earthly administrative units also bears upon the God-man question. One view, supported by a literal reading of the Bible, is that God created man in His own image. Another view is that man inevitably creates anthropomorphic gods in *his* own image. With either view, of course, the parallels between God and man remain. In this folk drawing, at any rate, it would appear that man has definitely created heaven rather than the other way around. This particular man-made heaven obviously bears little relationship to the concept of afterlife as defined by theologians. Moreover, in the parodistic context, a heaven as highly organized as the chart suggests would be more like hell.

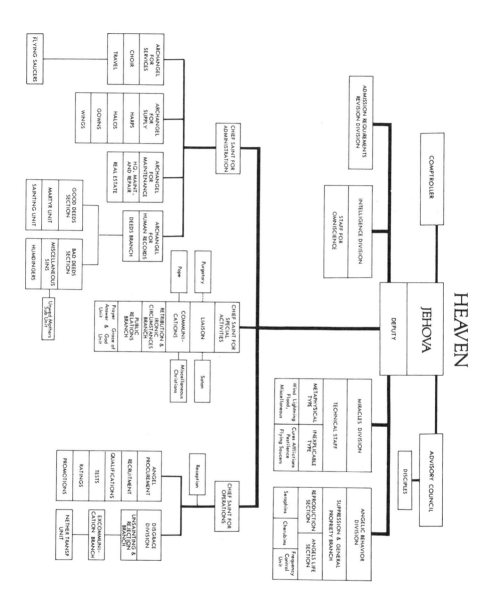

69. Project Swing

It is the impact of the organizational structure rather than the organization per se that is most striking in the modern-day business world. The most elementary matter or the simplest request becomes grossly transformed as it moves from one individual's desk to the next. The final result may bear little or no resemblance to the initial idea. This facet of the workings of the paperwork empire is imaginatively displayed in a series of related cartoons. Implicit also in this series is the marked contrast between theory and practice. Generally, Americans tend to prefer pragmatic and utilitarian principles, whereas they often mistrust elaborate theoretical formulations. In this instance, even the initial project sponsor had little idea of what was really needed by the prospective user to solve his problem. One has the feeling that many well-intentioned charitable and welfare agencies may be guilty of what this cartoon series condemns. The moral is clearly to consult first with the individual or group to be helped. Other versions of this folk cartoon show how the basic idea can be communicated by as few as two or three drawings or by as many as nine.

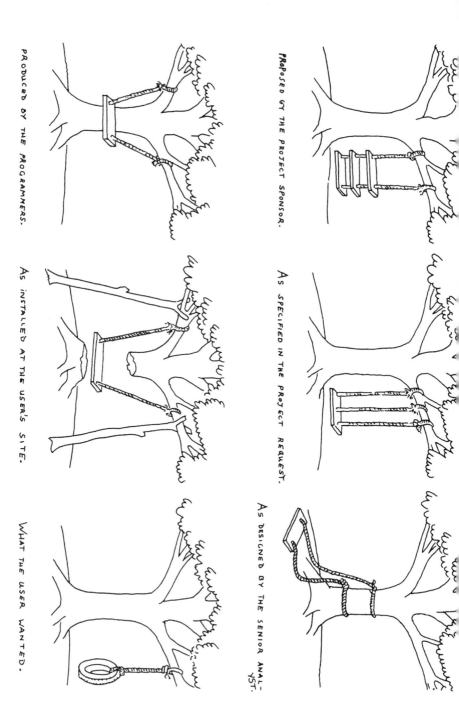

PROPOSED BY THE PROJECT SPONSOR.

AS SPECIFIED IN THE PROJECT REQUEST.

AS DESIGNED BY THE SENIOR ANALYST.

PRODUCED BY THE PROGRAMMERS.

AS INSTALLED AT THE USER'S SITE.

WHAT THE USER WANTED.

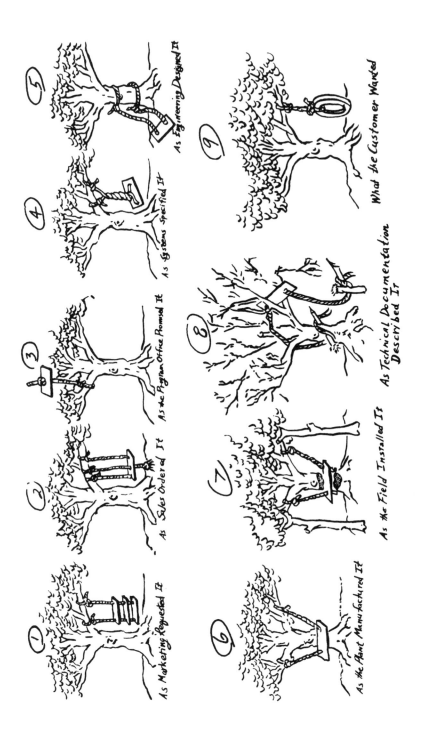

1. As Marketing Requested It

2. As Sales Ordered It

3. As the Program Office Promised It

4. As Systems Specified It

5. As Engineering Designed It

6. As the Plant Manufactured It

7. As the Field Installed It

8. As Technical Documentation Described It

9. What the Customer Wanted

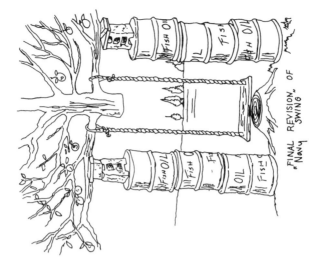

FINAL REVISION OF
"Navy SWING"

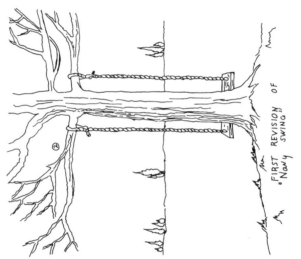

FIRST REVISION OF
"Navy SWING"

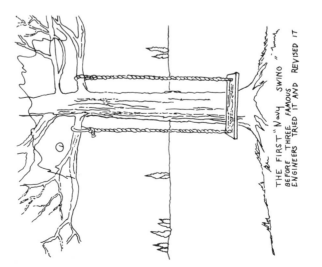

THE FIRST "Navy" SWING
BEFORE THREE FAMOUS
ENGINEERS TRIED IT AND REVISED IT

70. It's a Tough Life

In the numerous versions of a folk cartoon depicting a hippie couple seeking unemployment checks and other assorted forms of government aid, one finds the same curious combination of consistency and variation. The captions begin and end in similar fashion, but there are slight textual differences. The cartoon characters share such features as long hair and highly stylized costume. On the other hand, no two versions are alike. In the stereotyped view of college-age youth held by a large segment of middle-class America, student activists are seen as biting the hand that feeds them. Other facets of the stereotype include unemployment, sexual promiscuity, and a lack of personal hygiene. The following four versions collected in Washington, D.C., during the period 1970 to 1972 are representative.

IT'S A TOUGH LIFE

"I'll run over and pick up my unemployment check and then drop off at the university to see what's holding up my check on my federal education grant and look into my research grant check, meanwhile, you go to the free VD clinic and check on your tests and then go to the free health center to get my new glasses. We'll meet at the Federal Building at noon for the mass picketing of the STINKING ESTABLISHMENT."

"I'll run over and pick up my unemployment check, food stamps, job-training and placement check, then drop by the university and see what's holding up my federal education grant. Meanwhile, you go to the free clinic to check on your scabies and pick up my new glasses, and then we'll meet at the Federal Building at noon for the mass picket of the stinking Establishment."

"'I'll run over and pick up my unemployment check and then drop off at the university to see what's holding up my federal education check and look into my research grant check. You go to the free VD clinic and check on your tests; then go to the free health clinic and pick up my glasses; I'll pick up the food stamps, hit the drug rehab office and we'll meet at the federal building at noon for the mass picketing of the stinking establishment."

71. Pistol for Sale

Oral American folklore, as does folklore everywhere, abounds with examples of ethnic slurs. We find American folklore about Irishmen, Jews, Scotsmen, Englishmen, Frenchmen, and many other national and subcultural groups. In the 1960's, among the most popular ethnic-slur cycles were those directed at Italians and Poles. Curiously enough, though the slurs could be and often are considered genuinely insulting and offensive, it is also true that they are sometimes enjoyed by members of the groups in question. Thus, Jews may delight in telling anti-Semitic jokes.

In the anti-Italian/Polish cycles, stupidity is a common theme, often in conjunction with cowardice.[1] The same theme is expressed in a number of folk cartoons. In the following texts, the alleged stupidity is reflected in the design of a weapon. In one of the versions, there is an unusual reference to the Portuguese. The name of the pistol is a variation of the well-known U.S. manufacturer Smith and Wesson. The mention of a half-caliber heightens the stupidity—since the nearest actual caliber is a thirty-eight.

---

[1]Cowardice is especially widespread in anti-Italian slurs. For example, how many speeds does an Italian tank have? Answer: Five. Four in reverse and one forward—in case they're attacked from the rear. Another example: What happened two hours after the Arab-Israeli war broke out? Answer: The Italians surrendered. The difference between the "stupidity" trait of the Pole and the "cowardice" trait of the Italian is revealed in one version of the common "What are the three shortest books in the world?" Answer: *Italian War Heroes, Jewish Business Ethics,* and *The Polish Mind.* For further examples and discussion, see Alan Dundes, "A Study of Ethnic Slurs: The Jew and the Polack in the United States," *Journal of American Folklore* 84 (1971): 186–203.

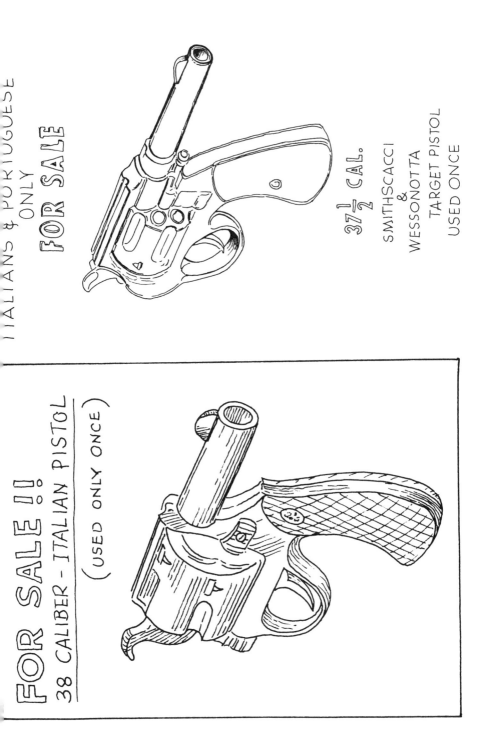

ITALIANS & PORTUGUESE ONLY

FOR SALE

37½ CAL.

SMITHSCACCI
&
WESSONOTTA
TARGET PISTOL
USED ONCE

FOR SALE!!

38 CALIBER - ITALIAN PISTOL

(USED ONLY ONCE)

FOR SALE

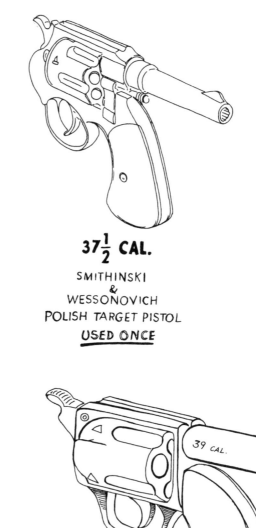

$37\frac{1}{2}$ CAL.

SMITHINSKI
&
WESSONOVICH
POLISH TARGET PISTOL
USED ONCE

39 CAL.

SMITHOVICH & WESTOKOWSKI
TARGET PISTOL

MADE
IN
POLAND

72. Heavy Artillery

A large bore weapon illustrates, in the first of the following three cartoons, the conception of military inadequacy on the part of Italians. The use of arrow or spear projectiles plus the word-play on "heavy" artillery further accentuate the stereotype of backwardness and stupidity. The obvious reference to hitting a large animal in the testicles to make him perform is a detail that occurs in a number of popular jokes. A second version changes the ethnic slur from anti-Italian to anti-Polish.

The third version of the elephantine weapon represents a localization evidently made for the Hughes Aircraft Company in southern California in 1969. The company was involved in the production of a heavy-artillery antitank weapon system. The system was called the Tow-G, which accounts for the label on the elephant's back pad and also for the labeling of the elephant's toe. Since Hughes Aircraft produces helicopters, it is appropriate to have one in the picture. Once again, the overt reference to the testicles is in accord with the previously noted tendency for employees to perceive hierarchical interpersonal relationships in sexual terms (as in being "screwed" by the boss). In American folklore, a set of traditional images suggests that an opponent is attacked in such terms: I've got him where it hurts, by the short hairs, by the balls, etc.

73. The Italian (Polish) Air-Raid Shelter

The following folk cartoons stereotype cowardice as well as represent the traditional phrase "to have one's head up one's ass." Perhaps there is even an allusion to the phrase "to not know one's ass from a hole in the ground."

ITALIAN AIR RAID SHELTER

POLISH AIR RAID
SHELTER

74. A Visit to the Butcher Shop

Among the numerous folk cartoons that might be adjudged obscene by some are the following depictions of a woman in a butcher shop. First of all, the phallus is referred to by the term "meat," a standard piece of slang that seems to have been omitted from the *Dictionary of American Slang*. (One phrase referring to male masturbation, for example, is "to beat one's meat.")[5] Secondly, the male fantasy depicts women as shopping for a penis or a sexual adventure. The cartoon also provides an outlet for male exhibitionism, a practice strictly forbidden by cultural norms. Third, the penis is free, perhaps as in "free love." Women who shop are normally interested in bargains, and the "something for nothing" philosophy is widespread in any case in American culture.

It is tempting to speculate as to whether the cartoons provide any support for the idea that some of the traditional meat shapes (e.g., salami or sausage) might be sufficiently phallicized so as to encourage sales from primarily female customers. The same advertising technique, after all, does seem to have influenced the shape and mechanics of women's lipstick devices.

[5]This phrase is found in the supplement. See Harold Wentworth and Stuart Berg Flexner, *Dictionary of American Slang*, p. 673. But there are other instances of this use of "meat." For example, there is the pseudo-mathematical formula: "The heat of the meat is inversely proportionate to the angle of the dangle" or its longer form: "The mass of the ass times the heat of the meat, with the catch of the snatch as a constant, is equal to the angle of the dangle."

75. The Roadrunner

The effect of motion pictures and animated cartoons upon American folklore is yet to be investigated. Among the folk cartoons that take as their point of departure a familiar animated cartoon character is that involving the character of the roadrunner. In countless technicolor cartoons shown both in theaters and on television, the speedy roadrunner is chased in vain by a coyote dupe. Just once, one might wish, the coyote ought to succeed in catching his elusive prey. In several versions of the following cartoon, the coyote actually does catch the roadrunner. Normally, when the roadrunner speeds away from the coyote, he emits a taunting "beep, beep," the only sounds he ever makes. The particular syllables, as well as the name of the bird, evoke the automotive arena where one can pass (after beeping one's horn) and thus surpass a rival. In this sense, the highway is a metaphor for the world in which speed counts and in which individuals are exhorted to get ahead of others. In two of the following cartoons, the normal power relationship is reversed and the individual who is ordinarily left behind and frustrated is permitted to sexually attack the front runner. Instead of the employee being screwed by the boss, he is able to screw his opponent. Obviously, great pleasure is derived from being able to quote the taunting "beep, beep" in a new context. In the third version, the normal role relationships are restored, and the roadrunner is homosexually assaulting the victimized coyote. Here, the implicit sexual nature of driving is made explicit.

76. Charlie Brown's Allergy

Comic strips have been even more influential than movies up-on the design of folk cartoons. Many male readers will remember having seen "eight-pagers"—series of eight comic-strip scenes depicting a well-known character, such as Blondie, Popeye, Tillie the Toiler, or Jiggs and Maggie, in a blatantly sexual adventure. A discussion of such materials belongs in a history of pornography in America. In addition to "eight-pagers," however, there are individual cartoons based upon a favorite character.

The comic strip "Peanuts" has become one of the most popular of all time. The characters of Charlie Brown, Lucy, Linus, and Snoopy are known to most Americans and to peoples in other countries as well. Television specials have been inspired by these lovable characters.[6]

In the folk cartoons based on Peanuts, the idea of the inno-cence of children is mocked. This stereotype of sexually inno-cent children (already discussed in the "Thank You from the Old Folks Home" letter) does seem to be false. In any case, the Pea-nuts folk cartoons prove to be most consistent in theme.

[6]The essential wholesomeness of the strip is revealed in Robert L. Short's *The Gospel According to Peanuts* (Richmond, Virginia: John Knox Press, 1965).

GODDAM YOU CHARLIE BROWN
I __WONT__ SINK IF YOU TAKE IT OUT!

GODDAM YOU CHARLIE BROWN
I WILL __NOT__ SINK IF YOU TAKE IT OUT.

77. A Folk Folding Rorschach

In addition to cartoons, other types of folk drawings exist. Several of these involve special folding in order to communicate their messages. The following series of blots look harmless enough, much like a Rorschach test. However, if the drawing (or a copy of the drawing) is folded in half and held to the light, an orgy is suggested. The very nature of the construction of this folk drawing is itself a commentary upon American sexual mores. Sexuality should not be overt. The superficial veneer of innocence and respectability must be maintained. Only when one folds the innocent picture as if to close it does the real purpose of the picture become apparent. Two versions of the abstract blot figures are followed by a silhouette drawing, which also reveals sexual activity when folded in half and held up to the light.

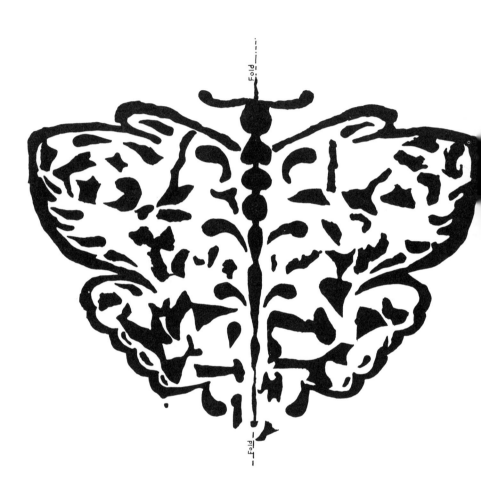

78. Inscribed on the Wailing Wall

Another type of secret message does not depend upon folding but rather upon changing the position of the text. If the following item is turned upside down, the pseudo-Hebraic characters reveal a classic retort in earthy English.

79. The Output Processer

Man's basic necessities do not appear to require the outlay of large amounts of money and effort. Yet, the first of the following two drawings implies that much of what Americans think they need are mere frills and superfluous luxury. It also explicitly attacks the product-orientation in the American worldview. Americans want to put out products in order to make it big.[7] Ultimately, the cartoon, which depends on folding to reveal the full message, is commenting upon the possible psychological roots of the American penchant for production and output. The final fold reveals a toilet. Note that the instructions for folding are themselves a parody on the "put-it-together," "do-it-yourself" syndrome so common in American life. Finally, implicit is a commentary on the American propensity for plans and planning. A blueprint or design is a first step in succeeding in business. If the design doesn't work, then it is typically "back to the old drawing board" for the would-be inventor. Both the "Output Processer" and the following "Jamb Detail" parody the American penchant for such designs.

[7]For a discussion of the anal-erotic theory of "making it big" or "making a splash," see Alan Dundes, "Here I Sit—A Study of American Latrinalia," *Papers of the Kroeber Anthropological Society* 34 (1966): 91–105. In this context, "How much (money) did you make?" is equivalent to parental inquiries about children's bowel movements! Folk speech does support the "money-feces" equation, e.g., to be filthy rich, to be rolling in it, to make one's pile, to have money up the ass, etc.

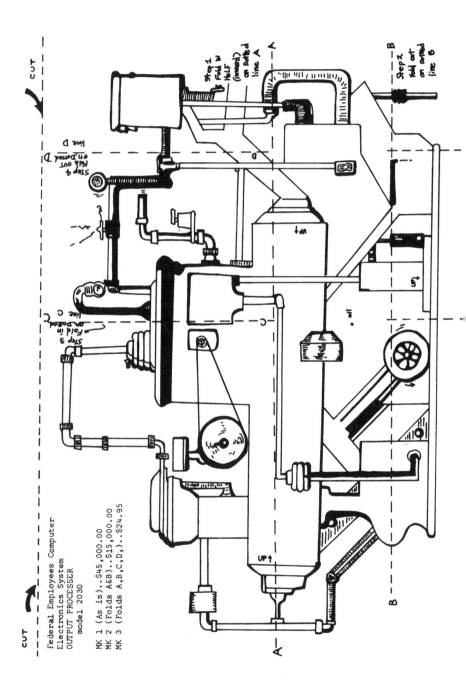

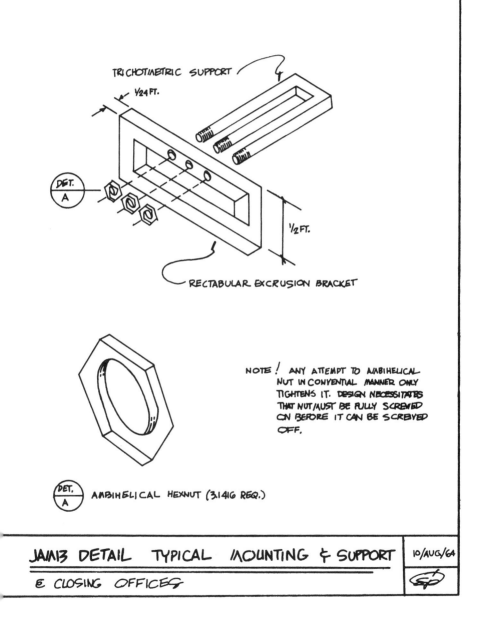

TRICHOTIMETRIC SUPPORT

1/24 FT.

DET. A

1/2 FT.

RECTABULAR EXCRUSION BRACKET

NOTE! ANY ATTEMPT TO AMBIHELICAL NUT IN CONVENTIAL MANNER ONLY TIGHTENS IT. DESIGN NECESSITATES THAT NUT MUST BE FULLY SCREWED ON BEFORE IT CAN BE SCREWED OFF.

DET. A   AMBIHELICAL HEXNUT (3.1416 REQ.)

JAMB DETAIL TYPICAL MOUNTING & SUPPORT   10/AUG/64

E CLOSING OFFICES

The Extended Double Entendre

Of all the forms of urban folklore transmitted by office copy machines, some of the most ingenious are those utilizing clever word play. While some of the shorter examples are in fact passed on orally, the longer, more complex ones lend themselves to mechanical reproduction and are probably rarely committed to memory by those individuals who read or hear them. A double entendre is, of course, a word or expression with two meanings, one of which is usually risqué. By extended double entendre, we refer to whole stories rather than single words or expressions.

80. Confucius Say

In order to appreciate the extended double entendre, one must contrast it with the more common forms of word play. One such common form in American folklore has been termed "Confucianisms."[1] In these pseudo-proverbial expressions ascribed to the

[1]For a discussion of this form, see Alan Dundes and Robert A. Georges,

great Chinese philosopher Confucius, one finds sentence-long double entendres. Confucianisms are in oral tradition, but long lists of them do circulate courtesy of the office copier. One such list is the following.

Confucius say:

Baby conceived on back seat of car with automatic transmission grow up to be shiftless bastard.

Man who lay girl on hill not on level.

He who fishes in another man's well often catches crab.

Wife who put man in dog house find him in cat house.

Man who farts in church sits in own pew.

Boy who go to bed with sex problem wake up with solution in hand.

Woman who cooks carrots and peas in same pot very unsanitary.

Kotex not best thing on earth, but next to best thing.

Man who marries a girl with no bust has right to feel low down.

Man with athletic finger make broad jump.

Squirrel who runs up woman's leg not find nuts.

Seven days on honeymoon make one whole week.

Modern house without toilet uncanny.

Woman who springs on inner-spring this spring, gets off-spring next spring.

81. Did You Hear about the Guy Who . . . ?

Traditional foolishness is as popular as traditional pseudo-wisdom. Another common short double entendre is the "punning

---

"Some Minor Genres of Obscene Folklore," *Journal of American Folklore* 75 (1962): 221–226.

rhetorical question."[2] Frequently this genre is introduced by the opening formula "Did you hear about the guy who . . ." The following examples are often attributed to Italians or Poles.

Did you hear about the guy who . . .

Spent four days in Sears looking for wheels for a miscarriage?

Took his expectant wife to a grocery store because he heard they had free delivery?

Looked in a lumber yard for the draft board?

Took a roll of toilet paper to a crap game?

Put iodine on his paycheck because he got a cut in pay?

Was so lazy he married a pregnant woman?

Felt so low he got his face slapped?

Lost his girlfriend because he forgot where he laid her?

Thought asphalt was rectum trouble?

Thought his typewriter was pregnant because it missed a period?

Wore a union suit because his wife was having labor pains?

Thought a sanitary belt was a short shot from a clean hot glass?

Studied for five days to take a urine test?

Thought Moby Dick was a veneral disease?

Thought a mushroom was a place to neck?

82. When the Japs Took Sal Hepatica

Having briefly sampled short double entendres, we may turn to more ambitious examples. The following item dating from the

[2]This form is also discussed in the Dundes and Georges article mentioned in the previous footnote.

1940's concerns defecation. In this instance, the effects of a commercial laxative are described using military reportorial language.[3]

FLASH! !
Here's the latest bulletin!!!!
It has been announced that the Japs have taken Sal Hepatica. The United States admits this, but doubts their ability to hold it. The latest bulletin states that the strain on the Japs' rear is tremendous and that they are evacuating all along the line. The Japs tried to suppress the report but it slipped out and they now realize the value of scrap paper. The U.S. got wind of it and reports the rear of the enemy will soon be wiped out.

83. Advice to a Stockholder

Similar in tone to the preceding item is the following standard letter presumably to be sent to corporate stockholders. Actually, this example could be considered a traditional letter. It has been included here because of its utilization of the double-entendre technique. It was popular in the early 1950's.

Dear Stockholder:
Our attention has been called to the fact that you are holding stock in the following corporations:

American Can Company

United Gas & Water Company

Consolidated Water Works

[3]One could argue that there are both phallic and anal aspects of military armament. Guns have phallic attributes insofar as they shoot projectiles and are identified by men as symbols of masculinity. Dropping bombs, however, could be considered as an essentially anal activity. To "dump on" someone or to "get dumped on" has a definite anal connotation. Further, "to knock the shit out of someone" is to beat an opponent unmercifully. In this item, the Japs have taken an American product that they apparently do not understand. American products are powerful, too powerful for the Japanese, who have had the "shit" knocked out of them.

Because of current conditions, we would advise you to sit tight on your American Can, let your Gas go, and hold your Water.

Also you may be interested to know that Scots Tissue touched a new bottom today and that thousands have been wiped clean.

Yours truly,

I. P. Daily
United Brokers Association

84. Insurance Companies

The influence of brand or company names upon folklore is well demonstrated in the following list of insurance companies. It dates from the 1940's but was still being circulated in the 1960's.

Something for all the insurance men of our group

First man sleeps with his own wife	That's Home Insurance
Second man sleeps with his girl friend	That's Mutual Benefit
Third man sleeps with a chorus girl	That's New York Life
Fourth man sleeps with his secretary	That's Employer's Mutual Benefit
Fifth man sleeps with the hotel maid	That's Traveler's Aid
Sixth man sleeps with an old maid	That's Prudential
Seventh man sleeps with the woman next door	That's Royal Neighbors
Eighth man sleeps with grandma	That's Old Age Assistance
Ninth man sleeps with anybody	That's Metropolitan

Tenth man sleeps with boy friend . . . That's Odd Fellow
Eleventh man sleeps with nobody · . . That's John Hancock
Twelfth man sleeps with
    Charlie McCarthy . . . . . . That's Modern Woodman

P.S. If you become pregnant from
    reading all this . . . . . That's Industrial Accident

85. Popular Brands of Bottled Beer

More common among brand-name-inspired folklore are those
narratives using beer or cigarette trade names. The following beer
story dates from the 1940's, and very likely some of the local
brands have disappeared from the scene.

Miss *Rheingold* was visiting the *Wagners* at the *Edelweiss* Inn.
She was itching to step out for a little *High Life*, so she tele-
phoned to *Patrick Henry* at the *Mound City Club* and made a
date with him for he was a *Stag*. They drove out to *Cooks* place,
stopping on the way under *Anheuser Busch*. He pulled up her
dress and when he discovered she didn't have on a *Red Seal*, he
untied her dainty *Blue Ribbon* and put his hand on her *Champagne Velvet*. Taking out his *Royal Six* which was much longer
and which he did not have to *Prima*, he took a couple of *Schotts*
at her *Schlitz* and began to *Progar*. She let a few *Blatz* of delight
and told him his *Griesedieck* was not a *Falstaff* but was of *Ster-
ling* quality. This pleased him very much, so he put the foam
way up in her *Atlas*. She went home that night *Extra Pale*, sad-
der *Budweiser*.

By *Ruperts*

86. The Cigarette Story

In the same vein are the cigarette stories.[1] The overtly sexual cast to the plots should not really surprise students of American advertising. The plain fact is that sex is used to sell cigarettes. What the folk have done is simply to make explicit the indirect, but suggestive, sexual references in commercial advertising.

One *Kool* evening in *Winston-Salem*, North Carolina, Miss *Pall Mall*, who had just flown in from *Marlboro* country, went for a stroll down *Chesterfield* Lane. She was going over to *Kent* to meet *Philip Morris*—a *Viceroy* from *Raleigh*—to go to the *Tareyton* Hotel for a *Lark*.

As they lay in an *Old Gold* bed, watching TV, she murmured, "It's not how long you make it, it's how you make it long." With that he popped his king-sized *L & M* into her flip-top box: and if she doesn't look like a *Camel* in nine months, it will have been a *Lucky Strike*.

But don't worry. *Philip Morris* was a thinking man. He used a filter tip. They said it couldn't be done, but it's what's up front that counts.

It might appear that anyone could make up a story line using cigarette brand names, but the fact is that traditional story lines exist. To illustrate this, we present a second version.

This is the cigarette story. One *Kool* day, Mrs. *Winston* took a stroll down *Newport* Boulevard, to the *Raleigh* Hotel. When she got there, she asked for Mr. *Philip Morris*, and the desk clerk

[1] In a brief study of the cigarette stories, Frank Hoffman traces tobacco pun pieces back fifty years to the period of World War I. See his "What's in a Name?" *Keystone Folklore Quarterly* 11 (1966): 13–19. See also Roger D. Abrahams, *Deep Down in the Jungle* (rev. ed.; Chicago: Aldine, 1970), p. 255.

said, "Call for *P-h-i-l-i-p M-o-r-r-i-s*." In a few minutes, Mr. *Philip Morris* came downstairs, and he and Mrs. *Winston* took a ride up the *Kent* elevator up to the *Salem* Room. And when they got there, the t.v. was on, so they shut off the program "*Hit Parade*." Then they got into the *Old Gold* bed, and he stuck his *L & M* into her flip-top box, and she said, "Ahh! It's that extra quarter inch that makes the difference." And he said, "*Winston* tastes good, like a cigarette should." In about six to eight months, if she's not walking along like a *Camel*, he'll have made a *Lucky Strike*—but you don't have to worry, because he was using a thinking man's filter.

87. The Seventh Race

Another elaborate use of names is found in the pretended narration of a horse race. The juxtaposition of the names of the horses in the running of the race provides the double entendre. This form of the extended double entendre is very widely known and expurgated versions have been commercially recorded from time to time.

The phallicism of horses and horse racing is an issue raised by this text. Some adult males enjoy identifying with a particular horse. The initial release of the horse from the starting gate is, in symbolic terms, the release from inhibitions of one's desires. The physical exertion of the horse, the lather, and the sweat all tend to suggest sexual activity. The object of the race is to outdistance one's rivals in the field on the homestretch and to cross the finish line first to victory and reward. In this connection, it is noteworthy that great racehorses receive the ultimate accolade: they retire to an "idyllic" life of stud service.

The significance of the horse for adolescent female teenagers seems to support the above interpretation. Many teenage girls become "horse crazy" and long to have their own horse. The unconscious motivation for the desire to ride horses after the onset of puberty would no doubt be emphatically denied by equestrian enthusiasts.[5]

SEVENTH RACE

Midnight Handicap	*Purse $2.00*
Eligible	16 Yrs. or over
Weather	Dark
Track Condition	Soft and Spongy

Entered	*Odds*
Passionate Lady	2 to 1
Bare Belly	5 to 1
Conscience	1000 to 1
Heavy Bosoms	6 to 1
Merry Widow	3 to 2
Jockey Shorts	50 to 1
Silk Panties	75 to 1
Clean Sheets	100 to 1
Thighs	125 to 1
Big Dick	2 to 1

They're Off

Conscience is left at the post. Silk Panties and Jockey Shorts are off with a rush. Bare Belly shows. Heaving Bosom is being pressed. Merry Widow is caught between Thighs and Big Dick. Clean Sheets is under the pack.

At the Half

It's Bare Belly on top. Thighs opens a hole and Big Dick is coming up. Heaving Bosoms is still hard pressed. Passionate Lady trails and Conscience is completely lost.

[5]For a brief discussion of horse symbolism, see Francis Lee Utley, "The Equine Subconscious in Ireland," *American Anthropologist* 66 (1964): 418–420. See also Thomas Gladwin, "Latency and the Equine Subconscious," *American Anthropologist* 64 (1962): 1292–1296.

At the ¾ Turn

It's Merry Widow between Big Dick and Passionate Lady. Thighs now working hard and Bare Belly is under pressure.

In the Stretch

Merry Widow cracks under the strain. Big Dick is going into a dive. Passionate Lady is trying to keep ahead. Bare Belly is close up and it's Big Dick over Passionate Lady by a length.

At the Finish

It's Big Dick trying to shoot out in front but Passionate Lady takes all he has and it's a dead heat, folks. Heaving Bosoms falls. Bare Belly is exhausted at the finish and Clean Sheets never had a chance. Conscience wasn't really in the race. Big Dick unexpectedly made a quick start and won by a hand. WHAT A RACE—WHAT A RACE.

88. The Game Called Bridge

If horse racing can provide an extended metaphor for sexual activities, so also can other games and sports. Even a card game, such as bridge, can be a vehicle. In the following text, the narrator is a Negro domestic who listens to her employers playing bridge. Her moral indignation at what she understands to be sexual depravity is of interest in the light of the history of American race relations. For one thing, Negro female servants were often victims of sexual assaults by white employers. Yet, these same employers argued that it was the Negro who was oversexed. This text then reverses the stereotype insofar as it is the whites who appear to be depraved. However, the text does confirm the traditional racist image of the Negro as a dialect-speaking, ignorant domestic servant.

This is called "The Game Called Bridge." It runs: A colored woman was applying for a new position. When they asked her about her former job, she replied, "Well, they pays well, but they is de most rediculous people I ever worked for. They plays a game called bridge, and last night dere was heaps of folks dere. Just as I was going to serve the refreshments, I hears a man say to a lady, 'Take your xxxxx hands off my trick.' Well, suh, I pretty nearly dropped dead, and then, bless my soul, I hears another man say, 'I got length but no strength!' I listened more closely then. A woman says, 'You forced me, and jumped me twice and you didn't have strength for even a raise.' Then another woman was talking about protecting her honor. Well, I gets my coat and hat to leave and I do declare before I die if I didn't hear a man say, 'Well, I guess all will be leaving as this is the last rubber!' Shore nuff, I got my things and left. I ain't working for such trashy people."

89. The Sex Life of an Electron

The following "Sex Life of an Electron" is a typical illustration of what is probably an endless number of localizations of sexual scenes cast in occupational jargon. No doubt the reader unfamiliar with electrical-engineering argot will need to consult a dictionary should he desire to identify all the terms employed.

Sex Life of an Electron
By Eddy Current

One night when his charge was pretty high, Micro Farad decided to try to get a cute little coil to let him discharge. He picked up Millie Amp and took her for a ride in his megacycle. They rode across the wheatstone bridge around by the sine wave and stopped in a magnetic field by a flowing current.

Micro Farad, attracted by Millie's characteristic curves, soon had his resistance at a minimum and his field fully excited. He laid her on the ground potential, raised her frequency, lowered her capacitance, and pulled out his high voltage probe. He inserted it into her socket, connecting them in parallel, and began to short circuit her shunt. Fully excited Millie Amp said, "MHO, MHO, give me MHO." With his tube operating at a maximum peak and her coil vibrating from the current flow, she soon reached her maximum peak. The excess current flow had gotten her hot and Micro Farad was rapidly discharged and drained of every electron.

They fluxed all night, trying various connections and sockets until his bar magnet had lost all its field strength. Afterwards, Millie Amp tried self induction and damaged her solenoid. With his battery fully discharged Micro Farad was unable to excite his generator. So they ended by reversing polarity and blowing each other's fuses.

90. The Law as It Should Be

A form of technical language that is somewhat easier for the layman to understand is the language of law. The following text is somewhat unusual insofar as there is a dialogue or, rather, a verbal duel. Also of interest is the fact that the female triumphs over the male who had tried to cheat her.

One evening after attending the theater, two gentlemen were walking down the avenue when they observed a well dressed, attractive young lady walking ahead of them. One of them turned to the other and remarked, "I'd give $50.00 to spend the night with that woman."

To their surprise the woman overheard the remark and turning around she said, "I'll take you up on that." She had a neat appearance and a pleasant voice. After bidding his friend good night, he accompanied the lady to her apartment and they immediately went to bed.

The next morning the man presented her with $25.00 and as he prepared to leave she demanded the rest of the money stating, "If you don't give me the other $25.00 I'll sue you for it."

He laughed saying, "I'd like to see you get it on those grounds . . ." and he left.

The next day, he was surprised when he was served with a summons ordering his presence in court as defendant. He hurried to his lawyer and explained the details of the case. His lawyer said that she couldn't possibly get a judgment against him on such grounds, but that it would be interesting to see how the case would be presented.

After the usual preliminaries, the lady's lawyer addressed the court as follows: "Your Honor, my client is the owner of a piece of property, which property she agreed to rent to the defendant for a specified length of time for the sum of $50.00. The defendant took possession of the property, used it extensively for the purpose for which it was rented, but upon evacuating the premises, he paid only $25.00. The rent is not excessive since it is restricted property, and we ask judgment to be granted against the defendant to assure payment of the balance."

The defendant's lawyer was impressed and amused at the way the case was presented. His defense was as follows: "Your Honor, my client agrees that the young lady had a fine piece of property, and that he did rent such property for a time, and a degree of pleasure was derived from the transaction. However, my client found a well on the property around which he placed his own stones, sunk a shaft, and erected a pump—all labor being personally performed by him. We claim these improvements to the property are sufficient to offset the unpaid balance. We therefore ask judgment not to be granted."

The young lady's lawyer came back as follows: "Your Honor, my client agrees that the defendant did find a well on the property and that he did make improvements such as described by my opponent. However, had the defendant not known the well existed, he would not have rented the property. Also upon evacuating the premises, the defendant moved the stones, pulled out the shaft, and took the pump with him. In so doing, he not only dragged his equipment through the shrubbery, but left the hole much bigger than it was prior to his occupancy. Thus, it was more accessible to little children. We therefore ask judgment to be granted."

– – AND SHE GOT IT!!! – –

(and that in legal parlance is what you call "splitting hairs.")

91. A Political Speech by a Woman to a Woman's Club

A classic example of the extended double entendre is presented in the form of a plea for women's rights. The following bit of imitation feminist propaganda partly affirms some of the conventional aspects of the female sexual role, but, at the same time, it complains about male sexual inadequacy. The text dates from the 1940's and has remained in tradition in the early 1960's.

We must have what man has. It may not be much but we mean to have it. If we cannot get it through our organization then we will get it through our combination.

We refuse to be placed in the gallery any longer and insist on being placed on the floor of the house.

We are willing to look up to man, but don't always want to be forced or held down without making a few motions of our own. We want to hold up our ends and show our possibilities whenever anything rises that fills our expectations. Nothing that comes can be too hard for us.

We are willing to work under men who have been above us in the past even to the point of exhaustion, if necessary, but are beginning to become disgusted with failings and short comings.

Never, when anything arose that required our presence and attention, have we failed to come again if the occasion required it, but too often have our hopes and striving been met with feeble performances that have left us disappointed and dissatisfied.

How often have our efforts to push forward with our ends been met with a cry, "Down with Petticoats!" and now I say, "Up with Petticoats" and "Down with Pants!" Then we shall see things in their true light.

As long as women are split the way they are, the men will always be on top.

92. The Birthday Gift

The confusion between a pair of panties and a pair of gloves provides the premise for an extremely popular extended double entendre. The present text dates from 1940, but it is likely that earlier versions date from the turn of the century if not before. All versions demonstrate remarkable stability, including the prefatory paragraph that provides the necessary context for the letter. Once again this item is really a traditional letter, but it is presented here because of its double entendre.

A young man wished to purchase a birthday present for his sweetheart. After much consideration, he decided on a pair of gloves. His sister accompanied him to the Ladies department to make the purchase. While there she bought herself a pair of bloomers. The packages were mixed up and the bloomers and the following letter went to the sweetheart:

Dear Little Sweetheart:

This little token is to remind you that I am keeping note of your birthday. I chose them not because I thought you needed them, as you are not in the habit of wearing them when you go out in the evening. If it had not been for my sister, I would have purchased long ones with buttons. They are very delicate, but she said they were wearing short ones in delicate colors. The lady I bought them from showed me a pair that she had been wearing for three weeks and they were hardly soiled at all. How I wish I could put them on for you for the first time. No doubt many other gentlemen's hands will come in contact with them before I have a chance to see them. Anyway I hope you will think of me every time you put them on.

The lady clerk tried them on and they looked very pretty and neat on her. I didn't know the correct size but I thought I would be more capable of judging than anyone else.

After you have put them on once, they will slip on very easily and when you take them off be sure and blow in them as they will be a little damp from wearing them. Be sure to keep them on while cleaning them otherwise they will shrink. I hope you will accept them in the spirit in which they are given, and wear them to the dance Friday night as I am crazy to see them on you.

P.S. Note the many times I will kiss the back of them during the coming year. Also the clerk said the latest style is to wear them unbuttoned and hanging down. This is supposed to give the wearer a careless look.

Your Loving Sweetheart,

John

93. Twin Brothers

In this double entendre, the effect is heightened by having a "kindly old lady" as the dupe. This is the familiar stereotype of the older person exposed to a graphic and protracted sexual description.[6]

It seems that there were twin brothers by the name of Jones. John was married and Joe was single.

The single brother was the proud owner of a dilapidated row boat.

[6] A similar text is found in J. M. Elgart, ed., *More Over Sexteen* (New York: Grayson Publishing, 1953), p. 152. The brothers are not twins, but their names are John and Joe. The plot and wording are nearly identical.

It also happened that John's wife died the same day that his brother's boat filled with water and sank.

A few days later a kindly old lady met Joe on the street and mistaking him for John said, "Oh Mr. Jones, I was very sorry to hear of your great loss. You must feel terrible."

Then Joe spoke up saying, "Well I'm not a bit sorry. She was a rotten old thing from the start. Her bottom was all chewed up, and she smelled of old dead fish. The first time I got into her she made water faster than anything I ever saw. She had a bad crack and a pretty bad hole in the front and that hole began getting bigger every time I used her. It got so that I could handle her allright, but when anyone else used her she leaked like anything."

But this is what finished her:

"Four guys from the other side of town came down looking for a good time and asked if I would rent her to them. Well I warned them that she wasn't so hot, but they could take a crack at her anyway. The result was that the crazy fools all tried to get into her at the same time and it was too much for her and she cracked right up the middle."

THE OLD LADY FAINTED.

94. The Wayside Chapel

A superb example of the extended double-entendre genre is the saga of the W.C. First of all, it plays upon the exaggerated modesty of polite society with respect to referring to excretory acts: it is embarrassing to allude to the bathroom. Second, the mistaking of W.C. for Wayside, or Wesleyan, Chapel, instead of water closet, suggests that for some individuals the act of defecation is a ritual one. There is a play on the word "regularity," meaning both church attendance and daily bowel movements. Other familiar themes include the embarrassment of defecating in public before a large audience. Another element concerns the social standing of the English lady (implying propriety) who is subjected to the detailed account.

Although often set in Europe, the text is extremely popular in the United States. One remembers that Americans tend to evaluate lodging on the basis of the number or quality of bathrooms. Despite their concern, Americans find it difficult to speak frankly about such matters. They may allude to "number one" or "number two" and ask discreetly for directions to the "powder room" in order to "freshen up." For this reason, Americans may well laugh at the fictitious consequences of a misunderstanding over such an unlikely abbreviation as W.C., which stands for "water closet." (It is of interest that the reading of this classic on a late-night television talk show around 1960 led to the show's being suddenly cut off the air.)

An English lady while visiting Switzerland was looking for a room and she asked a schoolmaster if he could recommend any. He took her to see several and when everything was settled, the lady returned home to make final preparations for the move. When she arrived there, the thought occurred to her that she had seen no "water-closet." So she wrote the schoolmaster a letter asking if there was a "W.C." The schoolmaster's English was limited and he did not know what "W.C." meant. Finally, he decided that the initials W.C. must refer to Wayside Chapel, so he wrote the following letter to the lady.

Dear Madame:

It is a great pleasure for me to inform you that there is a "W.C." located some nine miles from the house, in the center of some lovely pine trees, surrounded by lovely grounds. It is capable of holding 299 people and is open on Sundays and Thursdays only. As there are a great many people expected during the summer months, I suggest you come early although there is plenty of standing room. This is an unfortunate situation, particularly if you are in the habit of going regularly. You will no doubt be glad to hear that many people bring their lunch and make a day of it. While I would suggest your ladyship go on Thursdays when there is an organ accompaniment, many go on Sundays too. The acoustics are excellent and even the most delicate sounds can be heard by all. It may interest you to know that my daughter was married in the "W.C." and it was there that she met her husband. I remember the rush there was for a seat. There were two people to a seat usually occupied by one. It was wonderful to see the expressions on their faces. The newest attraction is the bell donated by a wealthy resident of the district. It rings every time a person enters. We hope that you will be here in time for our bazaar to be held very soon. The proceeds will go towards the purchase of plush seats which people have long felt are needed, as the present seats have holes in them. My wife is rather delicate so she can't go regularly. It has been almost a year since she last went. Naturally, it pains her very much not to go more often.

I should be glad to reserve the best seat for you, where you can be seen by all. For the children, there is a special time and place so they won't disturb their elders.

Perhaps when you are ready to go, we can go together. I hope I have been of some service to you.

I remain yours,

The Schoolmaster

95. George Takes Up Golf

The game of golf provides the context for one of the most elaborate traditional extended double entendres. The text depends upon the misunderstandings that arise when a man who knows nothing about golf attempts to play the game. The association of golf with sexuality is found in other golf folklore, as in the many jokes about "golf widows" in which a husband gives up his wife to play golf. In other words, playing golf is a substitute activity for playing with one's wife.[7]

[7]For representative scholarship, see C. Adatto, "On Play and the Psychopathology of Golf," *Journal of the American Psychoanalytic Association* 12 (1964): 826–841.

As a matter of fact it is our contention that a great many American games played primarily by males are based upon variations of a basic underlying paradigmatic pattern: namely, shooting or striking a ball with a club, racket, mallet, or bat into a hoop, cup, or goal area. This pattern seems to have definite significance in terms of sexual symbolism. (Note also such slang as to "strike out," meaning to fail to "score," that is, fail to have sexual intercourse.) It is also curious that the extreme anxiety in American society about male homosexuality is accompanied by a fanatic devotion to professional male teams who attempt to score by penetrating their opponents' defense.

It is noteworthy that the following text opens with a wife's suggestion to her husband that he take up golf, implying that she would prefer him to find a nonsexual physical outlet. The explicit homosexual reference in the golf lesson brings to mind the fact that golf is most often played by men in all-male groups of two or four. (A young boy usually carries the well-to-do golfer's bag of clubs and may offer advice as to how the ball should be played in order to sink it in the hole.) The lack of heterosexual activity in golf play is indicated by the last line of this double entendre in which "the flag goes up." In this context, this is analogous to a woman's "flying Baker" (a red flag), meaning that she is menstruating and hence unavailable as a sexual object.

George Takes Up Golf

My wife said to me, "George, it's about time you learned to play golf." You know golf? That's the game where you chase a ball all over the country when you are too old to chase women. So I went to see James and asked him if he would teach me how to play. He said, "Sure, you've got balls, haven't you?" I said, "Yes, but sometimes on cold mornings they're kind of hard to find." "Bring them to the clubhouse tomorrow," he said, "and we will tee off." "What's tee off?" I said. He said, "It's a golf term and we have to tee off in front of the clubhouse." "Not for me," I said. "You can tee off there if you want to, but I'll tee off in back of the barn somewhere." "No, no," he said, "A tee is a little thing about the size of your little finger." "Yeah, I've got one of those." "Well," he said. "Do you play golf sitting down? I always thought that you stood up and walked around." "You do. You're standing up when you put the ball on the tee." Well, folks, I thought that was stretching things a little bit too far and I said so. He said, "You've got a bag, haven't you?" "Sure," I said. "Can't you open the bag and take one out?" I said, "I suppose I could, but I'll be damned if I'm going to." He asked me if I didn't have a zipper on my bag. But I told him, "No, mine is the old-fashioned type." Then he asked me if I knew how to hold my club. Well, after 50 years I should have some sort of idea, and I told him so. He said, "You take your club in both hands." Folks, I knew right then he didn't know what he was talking about. Then he said, "You swing it over your shoulder." "No, that's not me, that's my brother you're thinking about." He asked me, "How do you hold your club?" and I said, "In my two fingers."

He said that wasn't right and got behind me and put both arms around me and told me to bend over and he would show me how. He couldn't catch me there, because I didn't spend four years in the Navy for nothing. "You hit the ball with your club and it will soar and soar." I said that I could well imagine. Then he said, "And then you're on the green." "What's the green?" I asked. "That's where the hole is." "Sure you're not color blind?" I asked. "No, then you take your putter." "What's the putter?" I asked. "That's the smallest club made," he said. "That's what I've got, a putter." "And with it," he said, "you put your ball in the hole." "You mean the putter?" He said, "The ball. The hole isn't big enough for the ball and the putter too." Well, I've seen holes big enough for a horse and wagon. "Then," he said, "after you make the first hole you go on to the next seventeen." He wasn't talking to me. After two holes I'm all shot to hell. "You mean," he said, "you can't make 18 holes in one day?" "Hell no, it takes me 18 days to make one hole. Besides, how do I know when I'm in the 18th hole?" He said, "The flag goes up."

THAT WOULD BE JUST MY LUCK

96. Proxy Papas

Our final example of an extended double entendre is set in England, and it involves confusing a governmental agent assigned to assist barren women with a door-to-door photographer specializing in baby pictures. In Americanized versions, the locus of the action is a Fifth Avenue bus, Macy's, and Central Park instead of a Piccadilly Circus bus, Harrod's, and Hyde Park. The use of what appears to be stage directions and dialogue suggests that this item may have served as a skit.

Among the many interesting themes in this classic is the tradesman who makes house calls. Much sexual folklore exists about such characters. (One of the leading characters of American folklore is the traveling salesman and his various adventures with the farmer's daughter.) The government also intrudes into one's private life. Here the government as big boss doesn't screw the man, but rather cuckolds him. This text goes back at least to the 1930's, but it is likely that the growing concern in the 1970's with overpopulation may make the initial premise somewhat obsolete. In the meantime, however, one must marvel at the cleverness of the composition, which succeeds in sustaining a most elaborate mistaken-identity situation.

In England, the policy of socialized medicine has been extended to include "Proxy Papas." That is, any married woman not having a child in the first five years of marriage must receive the service of a Government man, who will attempt to be the means of her becoming a mother.

The Smiths have no children and the Government man is due. Smith leaves for work. He has a hang-dog look as he pecks his wife dutifully at the door.

Smith: I'm off. The Government man should be here early.

He leaves as his wife pretties herself, putting on her most seductive dress. But instead of the Government man, a door-to-door photographer in baby pictures knocks on the door.

Mrs. S: Oh, good morning.

Man: You probably don't know me, but I represent . . .

Mrs. S: Oh yes. You don't need to explain. My husband said to expect you.

Man: I make a specialty of babies—especially twins.

Mrs. S: That is what my husband said. Please sit down.

Man: Then your husband probably told you that . . .

Mrs. S: Oh, Yes! We both agreed it is the best thing to do.

Man: Well, in that case we may as well get started.

Mrs. S: (Blushing) Just—just where do we start?

Man: Just leave everything to me, madam. I recommend two in the bathtub, one on the couch, and a couple on the floor.

Mrs. S: Bathtub! Floor! No wonder Harry and I never . . .

Man: Well, my dear lady, even the best of us can't guarantee a good one every time. But, say, out of six, one is bound to be a honey. I usually have the best luck with shots in the bathtub.

Mrs. S: Pardon me, but it seems—a bit informal.

Man: No indeed, in my line a man can't do his best work in a hurry. (He opens his album and shows baby pictures to her) Look at this baby. Took four hours, but isn't she a honey?

Mrs. S: Yes, a lovely child.

Man: But for a tough assignment, look at this baby. Believe it or not, but it was done on top of a bus in Picadilly Circus.

Mrs. S: My God!

Man: It's not hard when a man knows his job. My work is a pleasure. I've spent long years perfecting my technique. Now take this baby. I did it with one shot in Harrod's window.

Mrs. S: I can't believe it.

Man: And here is a picture of the prettiest twins in town. They turned out exceptionally well considering their mother was so—so difficult. But I knocked off the job in Hyde Park on a snowy afternoon. It took from two until five in the evening. I never worked under such difficult conditions. People were crowding around, four and five deep, pushing to get a look.

Mrs. S: Four and five deep?!?

Man: Yes, and more than three hours—but I had two bobbies helping me. I could have done another before dark, but by that time I had to stop as the squirrels were nibbling at my equipment. Well, madam, if you are ready, I'll get my tripod and get to work.

Mrs. S: Tripod?

Man: Yes, I always use a tripod to rest my equipment on. It is much too heavy for me to hold any length of time. Mrs. Smith—Good Lord!—She's fainted!

Conclusions

The variety of folkloristic forms that have been presented in this book clearly demonstrates the strength of urban folklore. We have not been exhaustive, but have sought instead to illustrate some of the major genres of folklore transmitted by office copier. We do not claim that all the items transmitted by this means necessarily originated recently. Unquestionably some folkloristic texts were previously transmitted orally or by handwriting. Nevertheless, some of these texts have been given renewed vitality thanks to the ease of duplication provided by modern mechanical reproduction. On the other hand, some of the folkloristic texts, especially those in office paperwork format, seem to have come about more recently as direct responses to the mechanistic nature of office bureaucracy. In any event, whatever the origin, the fact is that the materials exist and that they are likely to enjoy increasing popularity.

If one accepts these traditional materials as folklore—and we cannot imagine on what grounds they could be excluded—then one is forced to reexamine several basic premises in folklore theory. It has often been argued that folklore thrives only among unlettered folk. "Folk" was, at one time, a synonym for "peasant." In the nineteenth century, the folk were considered to be the illiterate in a literate society, that is, those people living in a society that had reading and writing but who could not read or write. According to the evolutionary theory of the day, as such peasants became literate, they lost their folklore. With this view, civilization and education were antithetical to folklore. Even today, many educated people are genuinely affronted when asked if they have folklore. Folklore, they argue, is something found only among lower classes or peasants. But they are wrong. Any group, regardless of its reason for being, can be a folk group with its own set of traditions (tales, songs, proverbs, games, slang, etc.). A campus community, a military unit, an office—each is a folk with its own folklore. If the materials in this book prove nothing else, they prove that office personnel—educated, *literate* people—have folklore. The notion that literacy kills folklore must therefore be rejected.

The literacy issue is partly connected to the old-fashioned idea that all folklore is orally transmitted. Folklore is oral tradition, conservative folklorists maintain. As we stated in the introduction, we feel that such a view is mistaken. There are many forms of folklore that are not orally transmitted. Aside from folk dance and folk art, which cannot be said to be orally transmitted, there is a whole set of traditional written forms, such as autograph book verse and graffiti (including the traditional writings on bathroom walls that have been termed "latrinalia"). These materials have not been treated here inasmuch as our aim was to investigate materials on paper transmitted by office copy machines. Nevertheless, autograph-book verse, epitaphs, flyleaf inscriptions, and latrinalia all underline the fallacy of thinking that all folklore is oral. Once the oral criterion falls, the whole question of literacy and its relationship to folklore has to be reconsidered.

Also related to the literacy issue is the question of industrialization and folklore. Do machines and advanced technology destroy folklore? We suggest they do not. Rather, technology and its effect upon human life become themselves subjects of modern folklore. Such machines as office copiers facilitate rather than inhibit folklore. Professional folklorists need to stop worrying about the impending death of folklore. Folklore is alive and well in modern America. Folklore will be around to help humans cope with their problems as long as there are humans and problems!

We have just begun to study the folklore of the machine age. Some of the items we have presented may well have individual authors. However—and this is the important point—the materials we have collected bear no sign of authorship. This lack of a known author is one good indication that the presumably original individual creation has been taken over by the folk and subjected to the folk process. The process consists of making the item a collective phenomenon, reflecting in part the values of all who share in the communication of that item. The fact that this type of urban folklore is absent from book-length treatments and standard anthologies of American folklore does not mean that it is not bona-fide folklore, but only that the definers and anthologizers of folklore had narrow vision. We have shown that many of these items have been in tradition for several decades. It is likely that antecedents for folklore on paper of the type treated here are much older than we have been able to demonstrate.

We suggest that a folk may be defined by looking at its lore. Rather than starting with an a priori definition of folk as rural peasant, we have chosen to examine a body of folklore and we believe that the urban folklore described in this book defines urban folk. Moreover, to the extent that urbanization is occurring throughout the United States—and the world—it is equally evident that the folklore transmitted by office copier is not likely to be regional folklore. We submit that the urban folklore we have sampled belongs to a large number of Americans. This is not the folklore of the Ozarks or the Pennsylvania Dutchmen. Anyone who has ever received a chain letter or seen a copy of Murphy's Laws posted on a bulletin board is a member of the folk to whom our materials belong. Urban folklore is one of the relatively few phenomena in the modern world that helps provide a sense of solidarity and group identity. While urban life may produce alienation, it also generates urban folklore to help make the ills and pressures of modern society just a little bit more bearable. We earnestly hope that the sampling of urban folklore that has been presented here will help provide a better understanding of modern urban America.